Praise for Clean & Green

'Nancy's enthusiasm and energy shine through. I love her holistic approach to cleaning and can honestly say I have learned loads from this book!'

Aggie MacKenzie, co-presenter,
Channel 4's *How Clean is Your House?*

'In *Clean & Green* Nancy is taking me on a whole new tour of clean-ingredient cleaning in my house. From daily cleaning to those more "annoying" home tasks, I found a new spring in my step around homeware. I learned so much from this book, inspiring more than a few ah-ha moments that led to sparkling results in my home without the use of any harsh chemicals. I particularly love Nancy's commitment to an eco-friendly lifestyle, small changes like switching to reusable glass bottles can make a huge difference for planet earth. Thank you, Nancy, for sharing your recipes for an eco-friendly home with the world!'

Jonathan Van Ness, of *Queer Eye*

Clean & Green

101 Hints and Tips for a More Eco-Friendly Home

NANCY BIRTWHISTLE

FOREWORD BY EMMA MITCHELL

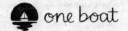

First published 2021 by One Boat

This paperback edition first published 2023 by One Boat
an imprint of Pan Macmillan
The Smithson, 6 Briset Street, London EC1M 5NR
EU representative: Macmillan Publishers Ireland Limited,
1st Floor, The Liffey Trust Centre, 117–126 Sheriff Street Upper,
Dublin 1, DO1 YC43
Associated companies throughout the world
www.panmacmillan.com

ISBN 978-1-5290-4974-9

9 8

A CIP catalogue record for this book is available from the British Library.

Illustrations by Mel Four

Typeset in Adobe Caslon Pro by Palimpsest Book Production Ltd, Falkirk, Stirlingshire
Printed and bound by CPI Group (UK) Ltd, Croydon, CR0 4YY

Visit www.panmacmillan.com to read more about all our books
and to buy them. You will also find features, author interviews and
news of any author events, and you can sign up for e-newsletters
so that you're always first to hear about our new releases.

For my grandchildren

Contents

Foreword

It's the summer of 2014 and a trailer appears on the TV that lifts my spirits like a kite. There's a particular programme that has worked its way into my yearly calendar and which I look forward to gleefully, almost feverishly. It provides escapism, gentle triumphs, human endeavour, tragedy without lasting anguish, the silliest puns to have ever been conjured and . . . cake. When *The Great British Bake Off* began, many thought it charming but, by this, its fifth season, it has become a much-loved staple in the late summer television schedule and commands audiences of millions. For a large proportion of the viewing public, *Bake Off* has become a beacon of happiness.

There, among the line-up of new 2014 contestants, is a woman with a bun of silver-blonde hair, an array of home-made bespoke baking tools, an irreverent attitude to the male judge and a significant eye twinkle. This person has a humbling ability to conjure delicious yet beautiful bakes. Her tarts are astonishingly neat, she slices her miniature sponges with a tiny guillotine that the Sylvanian family Marie Antoinette would flee from, and she impresses the judges week after week. Nancy Birtwhistle bakes her way to the final and, of course, on that significant day her diminutive afternoon tea components are perfection and Mary and Paul agree: she becomes the series winner.

I next encounter Nancy several years later, on social media, when her beautiful cakes appear in my feed. To my delight, she follows me back and we exchange tweets and Instagram comments now and then. The limitless energy, creativity and ingenuity that charmed those huge audiences and won her the much-coveted trophy, emanates from my phone screen. I marvel once more at Nancy's astonishing ability to create both beautiful edible designs and delicious, homely bakes from sugar, flour, eggs and fondant. Then, as her Instagram following builds, she begins to share more than just baked wonders. As 2019 begins, Nancy's tips for removing stains, cleaning a clogged iron and avoiding plastic waste start to appear among the pies and puddings. The sort of no-nonsense cleaning advice that for the most part fell out of fashion two generations ago, becomes a staple of Nancy's Instagram videos and stories. She shows off her sparkling sinks, bright white laundry and shiny oven shelves. Her wealth of knowledge is astonishing and I envy her gleaming surfaces.

There's a compelling and timely theme uniting all the household tips that Nancy shares. Each is designed to minimize waste, harsh chemical pollutants, single plastic use or adverse impact on wildlife. Nancy begins to give her followers recipes for home-made kitchen surface and floor cleaners, washing powder mixes, fabric conditioners and scouring concoctions. The environmentally friendly credentials and simplicity of each of her methods is compelling, as is the cleanliness of the drawers in her washing machine. Apparently, her home-made washing powder has made washing machine drawer gunge (I'm not sure there is a dedicated noun for this unpleasant greyish substance) a thing of the past. I eye my horribly gungey drawers with no small amount of shame and resolve to follow this sage advice.

Nancy's knowledge doesn't stop at replacements for big brand cleaning products full of pollutants though, she also has a hint of the hedge witch about her. In one of her wonderful instafilms she places her grimy oven shelves with baked-on spills in a patch of dewy grass overnight. Some manner of mysterious lawn magic takes place while Nancy sleeps and in the morning her metal racks are gleaming and completely free of stains. I'm agog. What IS this magical process? Is she the mistress of a band of lawn pixies? I'm fascinated. Next, she gathers ivy leaves, snips them into tiny shards and places them in her washing machine with badly stained white shirts. The grass-cleaning was one thing, but surely this coarse, leafy confetti can't have any effect on fibres ingrained with soil. I'm wrong, of course. Ivy, it turns out, contains saponin, a natural foaming detergent that can enhance the effect of Nancy's home-made washing mix on her husband's polo shirts. I studied botany, I'm a biologist, yet I have never heard of this and I reel. The result is remarkable: with some simple reagents and a few chopped ivy leaves she's achieved a white as bright as Tess Daly's gnashers. The stains are nowhere. Nancy's knowledge of natural ways to clean is wondrous.

Just this morning, as her daily Instagram stories appeared reassuringly in my feed, Nancy's knowledge comes to my rescue. I have a slow-emptying bathroom sink and have no idea how to fix it. Like a sooth-saying enchantress with a bucket full of bicarb, Nancy solves this very problem and, feeling slightly spooked as though she can peep through my telephone screen, I follow her instructions, water flows freely once again and I swear I can almost hear bathroom angels (and Nancy of course) singing a watery chorus. What a woman.

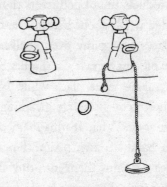

The world can be a very dark place just now. Our newsfeeds are full of terrifying, heart-sinking turmoil and a sub-microscopic, immensely clever virus that has turned our world upside down. Nancy, her writing and her Instagram: her optimism, crusade for cleaning that is gentler on the environment and, let's face it, her jaunty dance moves, are antidotes to everything. While scrolling through my Instagram stories I always pause to watch Nancy's daily clips. I learn from her constantly, marvel at her cunning ways with bicarb and secretly fangirl Shadow the rescue hen. This brilliant woman's warmth and down to earth approach brings solace to my feed. Nancy has blended invaluable snippets of lost knowledge with her boundless creativity to make this, a book that any householder with concerns about the environment should seek out. On these pages she shares her encyclopaedic knowledge of lo-fi, earth-kind yet incredibly effective ways to be more green while you clean. You're holding a tangible version of Nancy's accumulated household wisdom and it might just change your life.

Emma Mitchell, 2020
Author of *The Wild Remedy*,
Making Winter and *Made Well*

About the Book

When I consider the number of labour-saving machines and appliances there are now compared to fifty years ago, I am surprised I don't have more time on my hands. No longer do women find themselves spending all day Monday on the washing, Tuesday on the cleaning and not to mention the hand-making of bread, pastry and clothing. We now all enjoy a whole range of products and equipment which can speed things up.

Modern living, however, is starting to take its toll – our overconsumption of single-use plastics, harmful chemicals and a general throwaway culture have contributed to problems of global warming, the pollution of our planet and the non-sustainable use of raw materials.

WHERE TO START, AND WHY DID I WANT TO DO THIS?

I believe every single one of us can be mindful of how our actions are impacting the planet's health and well-being and, of course, I realize that if it is only me that's trying to alter my home cleaning habits then very little will change. I do believe, however, that if the price is right, if the recipes work and they are easy, people will make the switch.

Whenever I am asked why I wanted to do this, I have a vivid memory of my family sitting around the dining table, and that day, I think, became my catalyst for change. We had been chatting generally about climate change and the fact that it now seems all too real. We were seeing changes in the weather, poor air quality, too many chemicals being used, too much crop spraying, too many planes in the sky, and we were wondering: what on earth is going to happen? Then I paused for a moment and studied my own thoughts. I looked silently around. What struck me the most was the look of smiling, gleeful innocence on the faces of my young grandchildren and the realization that they were totally unaware of the plight our planet faces. I, too, appreciated that they will be the adults for whom the planet will be so desperately fragile if something is not done soon.

I knew that I already had a certain amount of knowledge of other cleaning methods, because many of the products used nowadays hadn't even been invented when I was a young wife and mother. My mission was to try to make cleaning completely green, effective and affordable.

Why bother? you may ask. There are plenty of organizations out there doing exactly the same. New green, eco-friendly cleaning products are entering the market all the time. They are good, they do the job, they are often packaged very invitingly – and they are often expensive! This book is for the people who want to make the change but in an affordable way. Nobody needs to spend more on cleaning products than they are at the moment. In fact, I now spend less! I list the ingredients required to make every single recipe in this book. I now buy my main ingredients in bulk – a 15g sachet of bicarbonate of soda is no longer any good to me. I now buy a 5kg tub, which is nearly ten times cheaper than buying it in sachet form. There are also smaller 500g boxes available which still work out at about six times cheaper than the sachets.

Please join me as I explain the ups and downs of my journey. I have made the switch – maybe you will too! Most of the tips have other applications, too, as my followers have shown. Why not share and connect online if you have found other uses for any of my recipes or methods?

LIST OF ITEMS AND EQUIPMENT

Below is a list of equipment and ingredients that are now my cleaning cupboard staples. Each time I worked up a recipe or tip, I made a note of the ingredients and equipment used. I am confident that you will be able to create your own clean and green home, make up your own recipes, following the instructions, and carry out any of the fixes mentioned in this book using no more than the items on the list below. I have left a few blank notes pages at the back of the book, because I promise you will want to add your own personalized applications for some of my recipes.

Followers occasionally comment that I am not wearing rubber gloves in my videos on social media, this is only because I can't operate my phone while wearing them!

Tools and kit

brown paper
digital weighing scales
measuring spoons
plastic bench scraper
rubber gloves
small plastic funnel
small whisk
wooden spoon

Containers, cloths and brushes

bathroom cloths – pink for the sink and blue for the loo!
dishcloths
dusters
fine wire wool
general cleaning cloths/rags
long-handled sink brush
old toothbrush
reusable glass bottles – with screw tops and spray attachments:
    mine hold 300ml – or, in the first instance, hold on to plastic
    spray cleaning bottles, wash them out and remove the labels
reusable make-up remover pads
sponges
tiny bottle brush
toilet brush

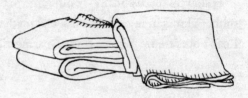

Kitchen cupboard

bicarbonate of soda (bicarb)
coconut oil
cornflour
grapeseed oil
lemon juice
sugar
table salt
vodka
white vinegar
xanthan gum

Liquids, soaps and powders

aloe vera gel
beeswax pellets (or soy wax as a vegan alternative)
Castile soap
citric acid crystals
eco-friendly washing-up liquid/dish soap
organic essential oils (I refer to lemon,
    lavender, eucalyptus, tea tree, clove
    bud, lily of the valley and peppermint)
green bleach (sodium percarbonate)
liquid soap
surgical spirit (rubbing alcohol)
vegan stain-removing soap
vegetable glycerine
washing soda (sodium carbonate)

SODIUMS

I thought I would add a little explanation about the three sodiums I refer to. I am not a scientist or chemist, but have done some reading around these three wonder products.

SODIUM BICARBONATE will be used a lot, and readers may know it as bicarbonate of soda, baking soda or baking powder. It is used as a raising agent in baking. (Baking powder is bicarbonate of soda with added acid to make it slightly more effective.) In essence they are all bicarbonate of soda, which is a must-have in our clean and green home. Bicarbonate of soda is a mouthful, so let us get friendly, shorten her name and know her as *bicarb*.

SODIUM CARBONATE is used a lot in this book, and although it sounds similar to bicarb (above), these two substances are not the same. It is not used in cooking and is not edible. It is a water softener, sink and drain cleaner and an all-round good green product. Rather than refer to it as a sodium, to avoid confusion, it will be referred to as *washing soda*.

SODIUM PERCARBONATE is an eco-friendly natural bleach which decomposes into oxygen, water and natural soda ash when it makes contact with water, making it biodegradable and, I have read, septic-tank safe. It is used in many eco-friendly detergents, bleaches and cleaning agents. It is cheaper to buy than many leading-brand products and does the same job. I regularly wash my dishcloths using a ratio of just 1 tsp to 1 litre of boiling water and leaving overnight. When referring to this sodium in the book I will call it *green bleach*.

REUSABLE GLASS BOTTLES

If you join me on my clean and green journey and you decide to invest in reusable glass bottles, rather than labelling them with paper sticky labels do as I have and buy a set of coloured glass pens. Write on the glass bottle which cleaning product you have inside and then, as an aide-memoire, write a summary of the recipe on the back of the bottle so that every time you need a refill you don't have to reach for the book. Multi surface paint pens are widely available and easy to use: just write it on, leave to dry and harden for a day. The paint is then 'fixed' in the oven by heating from cold to 180°C for one hour. The writing is permanent and will not wash off. I invested in brown glass bottles rather than clear because I have read that light can weaken certain ingredients once mixed. Alternatively, you may choose to invest in good quality, reusable plastic spray bottles instead of glass, which is of course a little risky especially when children are around. The contents can still be labelled with multi surface pens but with no oven fixing to make permanent, so you may have to occasionally rewrite.

Get creative – you'll be using them for years!

CHEAPER IN BULK

Starting out on this journey, I bought my ingredients in small quantities and, while still not terribly expensive, I found it so frustrating when I wanted to make up more floor cleaner or furniture polish only to find I had run out of this or that. I now buy my hero ingredients in large quantities – I know I can never have too much washing soda, bicarb, citric acid or surgical spirit.

Of these ingredients, there are those that can be used on their own for certain cleaning jobs, but reaching for a 5-litre tub every time is not practical. I keep a spray bottle of white vinegar handy – it makes the vinegar go further and is great for a direct on-the-spot spray onto a little limescale patch. I reach for my small bottle of surgical spirit (rather than the 3-litre can) to dampen a cotton pad to remove make-up marks from my favourite jacket. This prevents any spills and wastage.

Similarly, my bicarb is stored in three different jars. One huge jar with a spoon for those cleaning jobs where I will be applying it direct – stain removal, teapot cleaning and removing scuffs from my white shoes. Then I have a sugar shaker full, as this is a great tool for giving a measured daily sprinkle to clean my kitchen sink. I have a third jar, again a sugar shaker containing bicarb perfumed with dry lavender, cloves or cinnamon sticks, which I sprinkle onto my carpets to freshen and neutralize pet smells or fusty odours, which you can read more about later.

SHELF LIFE

I make up 300–400ml of my products at a time. Some last longer than others – spray starch, for example, I have for months, while all-purpose cleaner, fabric conditioner and iron-ing water I make monthly. The products don't go off, mainly because the ingredients usually contain vinegar and/or surgical spirit, which are preservatives anyway.

FALSE FRIENDS: BICARB AND LEMON JUICE

When embarking on my clean and green journey, online searches, YouTube videos and reading led me down conflicting paths, and I found that the only way to understand was to try things out. An established belief I had was that bicarb and lemon juice are great cleaning partners. I have since come to realize that they are great partners, but not together.

Bicarb is alkaline and lemon juice is a natural acid. OK – so far, so good. When they are mixed together they fizz, and this is where it gets interesting. I used to think the fizz was great: this was the natural cleaning process in action! Cleaning my bathroom, fridge, you name it. The fizz, it turns out, is a simple chemical reaction between the two. The fizzing gives off carbon dioxide gas and the white mass left behind is simply salt and water. In baking, this chemical reaction is perfect as that quick chemical reaction 'fizz' causes cakes to rise. Baking powder has the acid incorporated, which is activated once liquid is added. In cleaning, however, we need to keep the two ingredients separate for best effect: bicarb on its own to clean the acidic tannins in the teapot, for example, and acidic lemon juice on its own to dissolve the alkaline limescale in the kettle.

LAUNDRY

The modern washing machine is probably the most-used labour-saving piece of kit in the home and has long been part of everyday life. We all load it up, switch it on, let it do its work, unload the contents – and for me, this happens nearly every day of the week. I rarely gave a thought to what was going into my machine, whether that be the detergent or the fabric conditioner, and whether they were harming my garments, the machine or the environment.

I would regularly ring the changes when it came to perfumed products, and picked up various coloured plastic bottles promising me a fragrance of wild flower meadows or a spring fresh breeze! Happily falling for the marketing magic contained on the supermarket shelf.

However, living in a hard water area (that's what always got the blame), my washing machines tended not to live beyond around five years. I was told five years is all that can be expected from a modern washing machine, particularly as limescale is such a huge problem.

Back then, a few years ago now, my washing machine was in a sorry state. The rubber seal around the door had hidden pockets of grey soap scum that would catch on white sheets as I removed them from the drum, the detergent drawer was mouldy and when I pulled it all the way out of the machine, its housing was a complete disgrace. Mould clung to every corner, the little water inlet holes were bunged up and I really considered spring cleaning my washing machine an impossibility or not worth the effort.

It was time for action and, as it turned out, the starting point of my eco-friendly green and clean (but not twice the price) move to a sustainable, non-harmful-chemical way of living.

THE BIG WASHING MACHINE CLEAN-UP!

Before you embark on the road to a greener, cleaner wash yourself (and I promise you, it becomes addictive) take a look outside to the drain where your washing machine pumps out water. I used to accept that there was always a grey-blue tinge around the drain grate. I so wish I had taken a photograph. Once I had cleaned my washing machine and made the switch to alternative cleaning products, I noticed that the outlet pipe drain was – and remains – clean and clear.

How often do I need to clean the washing machine?

This is a one-off, and if your machine is really bad, as mine was, then this overhaul will probably take a couple of hours. Get the music on and enjoy the journey, because once you have changed to eco-friendly detergent and fabric conditioner your washing machine will not mess up ever again.

You will need

washing-up bowl of hot water
small handy bowl of hot water with 1 tbsp eco-friendly
    washing-up liquid/dish soap
375g washing soda, 250g to clean the detergent drawer and
    125g for a freshening wash cycle
white vinegar in a spray bottle
125ml white vinegar for a final wash cycle

rubber gloves
cleaning cloths
old toothbrush

Start by dissolving 250g washing soda in a washing-up bowl of hot water until all the crystals have gone. I find placing the washing soda in the bowl first then allowing the hot water to run onto it gives better results than adding the soda to the water.

Remove the detergent drawer of your washing machine completely. The fabric conditioner compartment usually has a separate little levered lid – unclip that too. Pop the detergent drawer and the separate fabric conditioner lid into the washing-up bowl and leave to soak for at least an hour.

Meanwhile, as the washing soda works its amazing magic, start on the detergent drawer housing. This is a steady, rather awkward but immensely satisfying job. With gloved hands, using an old toothbrush and white vinegar in a spray bottle, apply the vinegar then scrub with the toothbrush and periodically wipe down with a damp cloth. As the vinegar and your elbow grease come together the mould spots, limescale patches and every globule of undissolved detergent will clear and the compartment will return to its former glory.

Then, taking the handy small bowl of hot soapy water and a cloth, work at further cleaning the rest of the machine. Regularly rinse the cloth and don't be afraid to pull at the rubber seal to get into all the creases of the seal around the door. Have you ever discovered dirty marks and streaks on white sheets as you take them from the washing machine? This is due to soap scum build-up around the rubber door seal.

Once the cloth has been worked around every crease, then spray the door seal with the vinegar, getting into every fold. Rinse the cloth in the soapy water and work it around again – the vinegar will dissolve any further traces of soap scum. Rinse and wring out your cloth regularly if there is significant build-up.

There is probably a filter at the base of the machine. Pull that out too and give it a clean – you may even find an odd button or two as well as grey sludge. The filter on my machine is high enough for me to just be able to get a bowl underneath as a little water does escape when it is pulled out.

Can you believe the reason a friend once gave me for why she had bought a new washing machine? When I asked her what had happened to it, she told me it was no longer getting her clothes clean and that dirty marks were appearing on what should have been clean clothes. Didn't like to tell her she just needed to clean around the rubber door seal.

The washing machine makeover is now almost complete, and it's time to return to the soaking detergent drawer. If your washing machine was as bad as mine, and took longer than expected, you may find the drawer has soaked for longer than an hour and nearer two! The drawer will be easy to clean – the washing soda will have softened any mould and undissolved detergent and fabric conditioner. A wipe with a cloth and a light scrub with the toothbrush on difficult corners followed by a rinse under the tap should do it. A final wipe with a dry cloth and it can be returned to its rightful place. If you live in a hard water area, you may come across rough limescale patches on your clean detergent drawer. If this is the case, spray with the vinegar and leave for 15 minutes or so and the limescale will dissolve. Then just wipe clean with a dry cloth.

For the final clean and freshen, add 125g of washing soda straight into the drum, 125ml white vinegar into the fabric conditioner compartment and set the machine to a 40-degree wash cycle. You may wonder about skipping the vinegar in case it leaves a residual smell. I promise you there will not be a hint of vinegar at the end of the cycle.

I was, and still am, determined my washing machine will never suffer in this way again, because from that day on I have not used the commercial fabric conditioners and detergents that caused the problem in the first place. I also have to mention here that, following that epic day, I have not had cause to clean my washing machine. The detergent drawer is clear and clean, the rubber seal free of soap scum and there's not a speck of mould in sight in the fabric conditioner compartment.

I'm so pleased that I carried out a thorough clean of my washing machine that day. It opened my eyes to the fact that my washing machine was just one tiny example of the grime and damage I was unknowingly allowing to get washed out into the environment. That was reason enough to continue on my mission.

LAUNDRY DETERGENT

My washing machine was pristine, sparkling, free of debris and scum and I was determined to keep it that way. My laundry regime was in for a makeover! I recall a disturbing and surprising day when, out shopping, I decided to spend time reading the backs of detergent packs and bottles. Shocked to see that every single one carried the following statement: 'Harmful to aquatic life with long-lasting effects', I headed straight over to the limited number of eco-friendly detergents, only to find their price was much higher compared to the ones I normally bought. The red warning diamonds are there on the non-eco-friendly packs, but I for one hadn't comprehended the hazardous, harmful ingredients that are used, and not just in detergents and fabric conditioners. I decided to formulate my own!

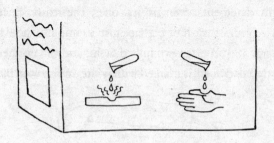

Do I need different detergents for different fabrics?

By buying the three items below (in the UK for less than £5 at the time of writing) you will have sufficient ingredients for at least twenty-four washes. That compares favourably with supermarket own brands.

You will need

750ml bottle of pure liquid soap (or see recipes for Ivy and Conker detergent on p.31 and p.33)

1kg bag washing soda

FOR DEEPER CLEANS

1 bar vegan stain-removing soap

or

500g bag green bleach – buy the biggest bag you can afford. It goes a long way and has lots of uses

PURE LIQUID SOAP Completely natural and eco-friendly. You may notice that I have not included washing powders or flakes among my detergents, even natural ones. The reason being that during a very short wash of perhaps just 30 minutes, powder and flake detergents can often not fully dissolve and the finished load, particularly a dark load, is marked with white undissolved particles.

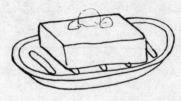

WASHING SODA You will be using this regularly throughout the book. Completely natural and effective as a cleaning product, laundry aid and water softener. Inexpensive and readily available in supermarkets and shops – this is a must for your cleaning shelf.

VEGAN STAIN-REMOVING SOAP There are many on the market to choose from for varying prices. I bought the least expensive, and to make it a go-to item on my laundry shelf, I like to grate it in my food processor and transfer it to a screw-top jar with its own little 5g measuring scoop. A little goes a long way.

GREEN BLEACH A natural whitener and boost for tough stains. This is essentially hydrogen peroxide in crystal form (a natural bleaching agent). A tablespoon added to the washing machine along with a tablespoon of pure liquid soap will do a great job on whites and tough stains.

It has become the norm that most of us over-wash our clothes. I remember a time when I had teenagers and they found it more convenient to toss clothes that had been worn for an hour or two into the dirty linen basket rather than fold them up to wear again later. Little did they know that I would retrieve the clothes, run an iron over them, fold them neatly and place them back in the cupboard. I do appreciate that there are times when clothes may not be terribly soiled but may smell odorous from cooking or simply from perspiration. A full-on hot long wash may not be required – the clothes just need a short wash cycle to restore them to their former glory.

There are also the hefty jobs. The football kit, the grubby

towels and the working overalls that will need detergent with muscle and power to get everything clean. I must also mention delicate fabrics: the woollen jumpers, the silky blouses and delicate polyester fabrics that are indeed our finest, most cherished and often our most expensive clothes.

Everyday washing

Starting with the everyday short wash cycle for clothes that are not too soiled – probably a mixed load of synthetics or cottons. You will need simply 1 tbsp washing soda in the detergent drawer and 2 tbsp pure liquid soap directly into the drum.

Deeper cleans

Our hefty jobs – the heavily soiled articles! You will need 2 tbsp washing soda in the detergent drawer, 1 tsp vegan stain-removing soap (or 1 tsp green bleach) in the drum along with 2 tbsp pure liquid soap – again, directly into the drum. I found a long eco cycle of 40 or 60 degrees (depending on the wash labels) brought these items up a treat – even the muddiest dog towels and gardening clothes.

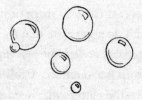

Delicates

Precious garments such as soft woollens, handknits, silk scarves and blouses can be washed simply with 1½ tbsp pure liquid soap mixed in hand-warm water. Even though there is a 'delicates' setting on my washing machine, I rarely have a full load, so prefer to wash by hand. I simply fold the garment neatly, lay it in the warm water and leave for 20 minutes before gently agitating then rinsing in lukewarm water followed by a tepid water rinse, then a final rinse in 1 tbsp of my fabric conditioner (see pages 35–7) in a small bowl of clean lukewarm water. I then transfer the garment to the washing machine for the shortest, gentlest spin to disperse surplus moisture before drying flat for woollens or on a rack or coat hanger for blouses, and so on.

Pre-wash soaking

An overnight soak in a large sink of cold water with 125ml white vinegar or 125g washing soda will loosen many stains, and if you take a look at any stain on a garment with wonder, not knowing what it is, how it got there or when then my advice is to soak first. If your item has metal buttons, refrain from the washing soda soak as it could tarnish them. Washing in hot water and detergent can fix stains, so much so that they are with you forever.

Worth noting also if you have a new, never-been-laundered garment and wonder about its colour fastness – a soak for a couple of hours in a washing-up bowl of cold water with 100ml white vinegar and 2 tsp salt added will help to fix the dye.

I used to be a fan of an overnight soak of cotton whites in

a weak chlorine solution. Chlorine bleach is well documented as being harmful to the ecosystem so I now overnight soak in green bleach. Just add 1 tsp green bleach to a large bowl and dissolve in a little hot water before adding your whites and more hot water to cover for an overnight soak, then launder in the usual way. It's brilliant.

IVY DETERGENT

Did you know that if you find yourself completely out of detergent you can pop outside and harvest your own? I have done this, once for fun and numerous other times, especially when my stocks are running low.

You will need

- 30g (a good handful) English ivy leaves (not young leaves, choose the older, dark, large ones)
- 3 tbsp washing soda
- fine netting bag that will keep the leaves in place in your washing machine

Wash your ivy leaves in cold water because they do collect dust and splashes, especially those growing close to the ground. After a wash, roll up the leaves and cut into thin shreds with scissors. English ivy is rich in saponin, a natural detergent and foaming agent. The purpose of bruising or cutting is to release the natural detergent from the veins in the leaves.

Pop the leaves into the bag – mine zips up – and then put the bag into the washing machine with your load. Add the washing soda to the detergent drawer of your washing machine. This will soften the water and help the natural detergent to do its job.

I am always surprised and delighted to see foaming bubbles in my washing machine when I have used simple ivy leaves. After the wash, remove the bag containing the ivy leaves (which are still intact, by the way, and smell gorgeous), tip them onto the compost and enjoy free clean laundry.

NATURE'S FREEBIES

CONKER DETERGENT

Did you know that the brown shiny conkers from the horse chestnut tree contain the natural detergent saponin? As a child, I was always excited when October arrived and I could fill my pockets with conkers on my walk home from school to then thread string through and play knock-out games. I am even more excited now to be able to collect a bag full and easily make my own liquid detergent. The following recipe makes sufficient detergent for twenty washes.

You will need

For 1 litre of liquid detergent

   130g horse-chestnuts (about 10 conkers/buckeyes)
   cloth bag
   hammer or rolling pin
   litre measuring jug
   1 litre boiling water
   tea strainer or sieve
   1 litre screw top bottle (maybe an old detergent bottle)
   hand-held blender
   5 drops lily of the valley or other organic essential oil for
       perfume (optional)

Pop the shiny conkers in a cloth bag or laundry bag then, using a hammer or the end of a rolling pin on a solid floor or outside, smash the conkers open to reveal the white centre.

Crush into pieces so that they resemble broken walnuts. The pieces will be uneven and that is fine. Alternatively, if your conkers are fresh, you can slice them on a chopping board with a sharp knife. Pop the broken conkers and any conker dust and powder from the bag into the measuring jug and pour over 500ml boiling water. Stir and leave 8 hours or overnight.

The next day use the tea strainer to strain off the thick creamy liquid into the 1 litre detergent bottle.

The conker pieces that have soaked overnight will have softened so pop them back into the measuring jug and using the hand-held blender blitz them to a paste. Pour over another 500ml boiling water and leave 2 to 3 hours. You will see lots of foaming bubbles from this second batch.

Strain using the tea strainer into the 1 litre bottle containing the 500ml made earlier and add 5 drops organic essential oil if you prefer a perfumed detergent.

To use
Measure 50ml in a cap and pop straight into the drum with clothes along with 2 tbsp washing soda (to soften the water) into the detergent drawer.

You can compost the pulp.

FABRIC CONDITIONER OR SOFTENER

I remember in the days before the fabric conditioners we now know and recognize, the normal practice was to soften the laundry water (in the twin tub) with washing soda to help make the detergent go further. Vinegar was always used in the final rinse.

Now, of course, we have our automatic washing machines which often have a dedicated compartment for the thick-scented, brightly coloured liquid. I have to confess, I was a huge fan of fabric conditioner and used it innocently – enjoying the variety of fragrances and promises of softness, prevention of anti-static cling as well as a long-lasting perfume. I was disappointed and surprised therefore to discover how, like the majority of detergents and cleaning products, fabric softeners also carry the standard 'harmful to aquatic life' warning.

I knew vinegar was a natural water softener and, on further reading, I discovered that it also dissolves residues left by soaps and detergents. With vegetable glycerine for added softness and a few drops of organic essential oil, I had the perfect recipe. I have been using this delightful recipe for over two years, varying the essential oil fragrance from time to time. There is no going back for me, and as well as knowing I am causing no harm to our waterways, I have had no return to a mouldy fabric conditioner compartment.

Do I need fabric conditioner?

I live in a hard water area, and I do believe I need to add water softener to the final rinse so that there are fewer creases in my laundry, it dries softer and is therefore easier to iron.

You will need

200ml white vinegar
15ml vegetable glycerine
20 drops organic lemon essential oil (or fragrance of choice)
glass bottle – I find coloured bottles are best as the contents are
    not light-damaged if left on a sunny shelf

The method for this recipe could not be easier. Simply add the three ingredients to the empty bottle, give it a quick shake and it is ready to use. Use 2–3 tbsp in the fabric conditioner compartment of the washing machine.

NOTE: Don't worry about the vinegar. The bottle of conditioner, once made up, smells divine. The vinegar is essential to break down any residual detergent, naturally softens the water, prevents static cling and will keep any mould from forming in the fabric conditioner compartment of your washing machine. The vegetable glycerine will soften fabrics and the essential oil adds the gorgeous fragrance.

Mixing a new batch of fabric conditioner is quick and even more convenient if you copy out the recipe onto the back of the bottle – either a sticker or permanent glass paint will ensure more can be made in seconds.

If you really are in a rush or have run out of one of the fabric conditioner ingredients, adding just 2 tbsp white vinegar to the fabric conditioner compartment will soften the final rinse water and there will be no vinegar smell on your clothes.

FLUFFY TOWELS WITHOUT FABRIC SOFTENER

For many years I believed that regular use of fabric conditioners and softeners were the secret to soft, fluffy towels. Long before I realized synthetic chemical softeners were not only damaging to the environment and were becoming quite costly, I learned that they can also create a chemical build-up in the densely interwoven fabrics of most towels. Over time these will make the towels stiffer and less fluffy. Similarly, too much detergent in the wash and overloading the machine will have an adverse effect on your towels.

Have you ever noticed that your towels feel soft and fluffy when they have dried outside on a windy day? This is because the pile has been lifted by the constant agitation of the fibres by the wind. The secret to soft, fluffy towels is as follows.

How often do I need to make towels soft and fluffy?

Every wash.

You will need

2 tbsp washing soda to soften the water
1 tbsp liquid soap
125ml white vinegar
a good workout!

Do not overload the washing machine when washing towels – give them space to move around.

Use washing soda in the detergent drawer – this will soften the water and clean the towels.

If the towels are particularly soiled, then add 1 tbsp liquid soap into the drum of the machine.

Add 125ml white vinegar into the fabric softener compartment. This will break down any residual detergent and soften the water in the final rinse. If you are able to line-dry your towels, so much the better.

Take your towels outside, hold on to one end and give each towel a rigorous shake – a tough workout! This will lift the pile, which will have been flattened at the final spin. Then, take your towel and turn it all the way around and repeat. In this way the pile is being loosened from all directions. Peg the towel on the line and leave the wind to dry, fluff and soften. Even if you dry your towels in a dryer, still give them a shake while wet – you'll notice the difference!

SPRAY STARCH

Why do I need spray starch?

For blouses and shirts with a crisp collar and cuffs, a neat crease in a linen napkin or tablecloth, or simply making dressmaking or craft easier for the seamstress and quilter by creating a stiffer finish to cotton. No aerosols, no hazardous waste and it is non-flammable.

You will need

1½ level tsp cornflour
200ml cold water
5 drops organic lavender oil (optional)
small saucepan
whisk
reusable glass bottle with spray attachment,
    or reuse a cleaned-out plastic one

Start by exactly measuring the cornflour into the small saucepan, then add 100ml of the cold water and, using the whisk, stir to combine. Place over a medium heat and keep stirring until the liquid turns from cloudy to clear. Turn off the heat then add the remainder of the water and the lavender oil, if using. Transfer to the spray bottle and use as required. The contents may settle when not in use, so give it a good shake before spraying.

Make sure your bottle 'sprays' rather than 'squirts'. Having bought my own supply of glass bottles, I noticed that turning the nozzle one way caused the liquid inside to squirt in a single stream, whereas twisting the nozzle in the opposite direction meant the contents were sprayed in a fine mist. Spray over your cotton collar or item so that the starch covers the garment lightly and evenly. Iron, and the fabric will dry immediately with a crisp, smooth finish. The addition of the essential oil leaves the items with a gorgeous fresh smell, too.

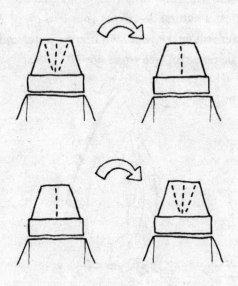

IRON CARE AND MAINTENANCE – INSIDE

If you have ever started your pile of ironing and then, when it comes to your best white cotton blouse or shirt, the iron splutters and spits and leaves brown stains, you have a limescale problem.

How often do I need to descale my iron?

If you live in a hard water area and, like me, you tend to fill your steam iron with tap water (rather than distilled water), then limescale will build up on the inside. To keep it at bay I would suggest a natural descale of your iron every six to eight weeks. Better still, make your own ironing water and your iron will not scale up again (see pages 46–7).

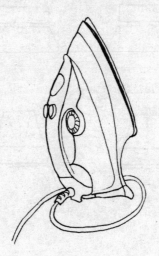

You will need

125ml water
125ml lemon juice
an old towel

Check that your iron is designed to be successfully descaled.
I believe there are models on the market that do not need
descaling – check your manufacturer's handbook or look it up
online if in doubt.

With the iron unplugged, start by filling up the water chamber to the 'full' mark, then tip the water out into a measuring
jug to determine your iron's water capacity. My iron holds
250ml water. According to the capacity of your iron, make up
a solution of half water and half lemon juice.

Pour this natural limescale remover into the iron, then plug
it in and switch on the electricity. As the iron heats up it will
splutter. At that point, lay it plate down onto the old towel,
allowing it to splutter and steam. Turn off the power and leave
the iron in this position overnight. The next day pour away the
water, refill with fresh water and turn on your iron. You will see
the steam jets are clear and clean of limescale. Your iron will be
working at full steam!

IRON CARE AND MAINTENANCE – OUTSIDE

Let us assume the worst-case scenario! Your iron was too hot yet you dived onto your best dark blue polyester blouse sleeve with it. Yes – I did that! The blouse no longer has a sleeve – most of it is shrivelled up on the plate of your iron. The blouse is ruined but the iron, thankfully, is not.

How often do I need to clean my iron's plate?

If you accidentally scorch an item or, at worst, take a piece out of a polyester garment, immediate action is necessary. Otherwise a periodic clean when the iron plate appears discoloured.

You will need

1–2 tbsp bicarb in a small bowl
wooden spoon or spatula
cotton cloth

First, take a wooden spatula or spoon. Don't be tempted to use a plastic or metal one. The plastic will melt and the metal one will severely scratch and damage the plate.

Plug in the iron and turn it on, and once it gets to temperature, turn it off at the plug. Using the wooden spatula or spoon, gently rub away at the black burnt-on plastic. It looks and behaves like chewing gum – stretchy and sticky. If you have a heavily burnt-on problem, then as the iron cools the plastic will refuse to move, so it is necessary to switch on the heat again and repeat. Slowly but surely you will have removed the unsightly gum and will probably be left with brown scorch marks on the iron plate.

Leave the iron to cool completely then simply take a soft cotton cloth slightly dampened with water and dip it into the bowl of bicarb. Rub away at the scorch with the cloth, taking care to avoid the steam holes, and you will see the scorch disappears readily. Wipe off any residual powder then polish with a duster. Your iron is as good as new again – but you might need to replace the blouse.

NATURE'S FREEBIES

RAINWATER: EASY IRONING
AND EASY ON THE IRON

When my iron needed replacing after a long life, I decided I'd make an extra effort to look after the new one and refrain from using tap water to fill the steam cavity. Tap water in my area, I have found to my personal cost, does create limescale build-up and deterioration to the inside of my iron. There are plastic bottles of perfumed ironing water on the market which will, it is promised, make your ironing a pleasing experience while at the same time preventing any damage to your iron on the inside. I looked at the ingredients contained in these bottles and couldn't pronounce, spell or comprehend any of them.

I decided I could make a natural ironing water for an absolute fraction of the cost because Mother Nature had provided me with the main ingredient – rainwater. Capturing rainwater that runs off the house and greenhouse for watering houseplants, seedlings and my vegetable garden has been part of my routine for many years. I decided to use this water to make my ironing water, too.

How often do I need to make up ironing water?

Make half or one litre at a time (depending how often your iron is used), and use every time the iron is filled.

You will need

20 drops organic essential oil (lily of the valley or lavender are
    perfect)
2 tbsp cheap vodka or surgical spirit
1 litre rainwater
1 litre storage bottle
large saucepan
funnel

Start by measuring the essential oil perfume into the storage
bottle, then add the vodka or surgical spirit. This helps to emulsify the oil with the water. Bring the rainwater to the boil in
the saucepan and bubble for just 30 seconds, leave to cool then
funnel into the bottle of oil and alcohol. Give it a shake and fill
your iron as appropriate. This recipe makes sufficient liquid to
fill a standard iron four times.

Ironing is easier with a jet of steam – creases are smoothed
out quickly, the natural rainwater protects your iron from
limescale and a floral fragrance adds a fresh finish to your clean
laundry.

SPOT-CLEANING COLLARS AND CUFFS

It has become a hobby of mine to regularly peruse the detergent aisles in supermarkets and to continue to be surprised at the range of products and their amazing prices that are said to do what can so easily be done at home naturally and cheaply. Take stain removers for collars and cuffs, for example. There are bars, sprays, aerosols and liquids all promising clean collars and cuffs. Thankfully I have never been tempted and continue to do the same as my grandmother did. Even though my grandad's job was working among industrial boilers and heating systems, he still wore a collared shirt every day. Similarly, my children wore a clean white cotton shirt for school every day, yet I swear their collars were filthier after a day at school than my grandad's shirt, even though he had been de-coking a boiler all day!

How often do I need to spot-clean collars and cuffs?

As required, though I always check school shirts and work shirts, and also white shirts and blouses.

You will need

eco-friendly washing-up liquid/dish soap

Simply lay the shirt out with the soiled collar and cuffs flat and facing out. Squeeze a stream of eco-friendly washing-up liquid along the dirt lines. Rub it in with the finger then leave for 10 minutes before popping the shirt into the washing machine on its usual cycle.

Washing-up liquid is fantastic at tackling grease stains – your soiled collars and cuffs will be perfectly clean.

REMOVING BLOODSTAINS

Bloodstains can be difficult and stubborn, but do not be tempted to buy branded products when you can sort out the job yourself without spending a penny. The job can be done naturally: no sprays, no chlorine bleach and definitely no boiling!

How often do I need to remove bloodstains?

As required, although the sooner the better.

You will need

cold water
table salt
green bleach, as a last resort
saucepan

FRESH BLOODSTAINS These are by far the easiest to deal with, but, as with any bloodstain, the golden rule is that hot water is your enemy. Sometimes instinctively we reach for hot soapy water, but when dealing with blood spills, the hot water will fix the stain into the fabric and make it nearly impossible to remove.

Immediately you detect a fresh blood mark, place the garment, sheet or pillowcase in a bowl of cold water. You will see the blood lift straight away, and the most you will be left with is maybe an outline which will disappear once you gently rub the fabric. Once the stain is gone, wash the item in the usual way.

DRIED BLOODSTAINS It may not always be practical or convenient to deal with a fresh bloodstain and a dried-in bloodstain has to be tackled.

If the stain is on a garment, sheet or pillowcase then soak the stain in cold water and it will fade in colour but will be unlikely to disappear. Take simple table salt and sprinkle it over the wet stain. Gently and continuously rub with your finger to create a paste with the salt and water. That should be enough to lift the stain. Take your time and it will fade. I then leave the garment for half an hour before popping it into the washing machine on a cool 30-degree cycle. Again, hot water is the enemy – a hot wash could fix any residual blood into the fabric.

OLD, WASHED-IN AND FIXED BLOODSTAINS There are those times when a blood spot may have been missed, and as you examine your pile of ironing there is a white shirt with a blood spot well and truly fixed after washing. I have to confess I used to reach for the chlorine bleach bottle to 'bleach' out the offending stain. Not only did this not always work, if used on artificial fibres the bleach can actually leave a yellow stain not too different to the bloodstain, and too much bleach and there is a hole burnt in my shirt! Chlorine bleach is a thing of the past in my house, so I needed to look for alternatives.

I have found that a strong cold salt solution works well. In a small saucepan place 3 tbsp table salt and 3 tbsp water, place over the heat and stir until the salt dissolves. Allow the solution to cool completely. Use this cold, very concentrated liquid to dab onto the fixed stain.

This method is particularly helpful if you have bloodstains, fresh or dried, on an item that it is not possible to cold-water soak. A follower of mine had a badly stained mattress resulting from a leg wound and I suggested she tried this. It worked a treat.

As a last resort, I have found that old, fixed bloodstains can be removed using a dab of green bleach. Dissolve ½ a tsp in 100ml hot water and apply directly onto the fixed stain, re-applying as needed until the stain is removed. Rinse away with cold water or pop into the washing machine. Green bleach is a natural, eco-friendly alternative. It is a great bleaching agent, and unlike chlorine bleach breaks down into water and oxygen molecules.

WHITEN THOSE YELLOWED WHITES

When I commenced my green expedition, I expected tasks around laundry to be the troublesome ones, and looked for replacements for whiteners. Whites need to be white, and my old way would be an overnight soak in a chlorine bleach solution followed by a hot wash cycle using a biological detergent. There are products on the market, some of which I purchased in the past, specifically targeted at whitening those yellow whites. I prohibited myself from using any of these products, and had to look for a natural alternative. By the time I worked up this little tip, my knowledge was starting to build and I figured I had an answer.

How often do I need to whiten yellowed whites?

Whites will yellow either through staining or not being washed separately, and I have even had old linens and cottons that have stained yellow although they were folded and stored away. This is really a one-off treatment for cotton, linens and other robust natural fibres, but it can be repeated as and when necessary.

You will need

3 tbsp table salt
3 tbsp citric acid
600ml hot water

large bowl
sunny day

Changing the bed linen one day, I noticed the cotton pillow protectors I use (cotton slips that fit easily over the pillow and underneath the pillowcase and will add a degree of protection and a longer life to your pillow) had yellowed. Hair oil and perspiration were probably the culprits, and the offending pillow protectors were removed and washed. Sadly, following a thorough 60-degree cotton wash, the pillow protectors, while obviously clean, were still yellow.

Before drying the pillow protectors, I got to work.

Make sure the yellowed items are clean before treating. In a bowl large enough to accommodate the items place the table salt and citric acid, then add 600ml of hot water from the kettle. Stir around with a wooden spoon until the salt and citric acid crystals dissolve, then submerge the yellowed white items.

Leave the items to soak for 20 minutes until all or most of the liquid has been absorbed.

Take the bowl outside into the sunshine, lift the dripping pillow protectors or yellowed items out of the solution and peg them to a washing line or rack in the full sun.

The results are absolutely astounding. The yellowing completely bleaches out of cotton, linen and other robust natural fibres and in my case the dried pillow protectors were crisp and white and returned to their former glory and no harmful chemicals were used.

You may want to rinse the whitened items in water and dry them again if you wish to rid the fabric of any salts.

No chlorine bleach or biological washing detergents required!

CLEAN, SANITIZE AND WHITEN CLOTHS

I adore fresh white cotton dishcloths and flannels, but they can soon become grubby-looking, smelly and unhygienic. I used to routinely soak my cloths overnight in chlorine bleach, not even thinking or considering the impact my efforts were having on the environment.

The choices I had were to either throw away my dishcloths regularly and replace, or boil them in the old-fashioned way in order to freshen, whiten and remove germs. Throwing cotton cloths away is wasteful, and was really going against the grain if I was working towards a more sustainable lifestyle, yet boiling cloths in a saucepan or washing machine seemed somewhat energy-excessive – until I considered the microwave.

How often do I need to clean, sanitize and whiten dishcloths?

Alternate days, or when required.

You will need

2 tbsp washing soda
½ tsp green bleach
500ml hot water, or enough to cover the dishcloth
large glass microwave-proof bowl
plate large enough to cover the bowl
1 grubby dishcloth or face flannel

This job is best done at the end of the working day. Weigh or spoon the washing soda and green bleach into a roomy bowl. Pour over the hot water, which will come about a third of the way up the bowl. Pop your wet dishcloth into the solution and make sure it is submerged. Place a plate over the top and microwave on high for 1–2 minutes or until you see the water in the bowl is bubbling and boiling. Turn the wattage of the microwave down to just 100 watts and microwave for a further 30 minutes. In effect, the cloth is being brought to the boil and is then simmering for the remainder of the time.

The plate and bowl will be very hot, but rather than risk burning yourself, simply leave the cloth in the bowl, still in the microwave, to soak overnight. The next morning simply rinse the cloth in cold water.

Your cloths will be returned to their former glory. I like my face flannels and reusable cotton make-up pads to be super-white, and this is a fantastic, fuss-free way to eradicate any make-up stains.

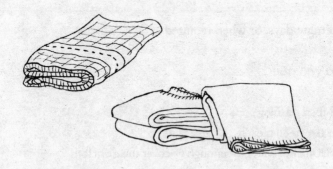

The energy saved by using the microwave for boiling cloths can be as high as 90% compared to boiling on the hob but, if you don't have a microwave, then boiling a cloth in a pan and simmering for half an hour will do the job in the old-fashioned, yet very effective way too.

If the weather is fine, and even better if the sun is shining, peg the cloth out on the line to air-dry. The sunshine will finish the whitening off a treat.

NOTE: To prevent a cloth from becoming smelly, after using, rather than leave it on the side of the sink scrunched up, open it out and leave it to hang over a plastic bowl or tap so that the air can circulate and it will dry with no lingering smell.

For a really quick whitening, sanitizing and freshen add 1 tsp green bleach to a bowl, pop in your grubby cloth and pour over sufficient boiling water to cover (about 400ml). Leave just 30 minutes and, once cool enough to handle, rinse and you're good to go!

REMOVE LILY POLLEN STAINS FROM CLOTHING, CARPETS AND FURNISHINGS

Lily plants and cut flowers are absolutely adorable, and the flowers are included in many sprays and bouquets. Their pollen, however, can be responsible for permanent staining all around the home – on clothing, furnishings, upholstery and carpets. Just gently brush past one of the magnificent flowers and the pollen can leave a permanent brown or orange stain on your best white blouse or shirt.

Prevention is better than cure, and removing the delicate pollen-loaded stamen as soon as the lily opens will avert any disaster. I take a small pair of scissors and a bowl and gently cut the stamen and let it fall into the bowl. I do not handle the stamens at all for fear of spreading the pollen onto the petals, as it stains those too.

How often do I need to remove lily pollen stains?

Even though prevention is better than cure, accidents do happen.

You will need

surgical spirit
eco-friendly washing-up liquid/dish soap
soft wooden-handled pastry brush (not a plastic one)
cotton pad(s) or clean cloth

A lily pollen stain can be removed if handled correctly. First, do not be tempted to rub it or pop it straight into the washing machine – both can fix the stain permanently.

Gently brush the pollen or vacuum (if it is on carpet or furniture) to remove as much powder as possible. Even a strip of sticky tape can be used to carefully lift the powder if it is in a place where it cannot be brushed off. Then take a cotton pad or clean cloth and gently dab with surgical spirit. This should remove most of the stain, but if there is a residual mark then a damp cloth with a drop of eco-friendly washing-up liquid (clear, not green) massaged into the stain will lift it.

If a pollen stain is on clothing and has been rubbed in and has stained, it can be removed. You will need two reusable cotton pads. Lay one pad under the part of the garment with the stain. If it is a sleeve, then lay the cotton pad between the two layers and use a hand to protect the non-stained part of the sleeve. Use a second cotton pad soaked with surgical spirit to gently dab at the stain. The pollen stain will transfer from the garment onto the dry cotton pad underneath.

This method has also been useful for removing ink, biro and marker pen from clothing and fabrics.

GET RID OF NASTY SMELLS ON CLOTHES

I have included this tip because spills of petrol and turpentine substitute do happen. Not often, but when they do the smell is strong and difficult to get rid of from the hands, never mind clothing. Similarly, garden bonfire smoke and cigarette smoke can linger on clothing long after the smoky situation has disappeared. This tip is suitable for unwanted smoke (cigarette or bonfire), petrol, white spirit or turpentine substitute smells.

How often do I need to remove the smell of smoke, petrol, white spirit or turpentine substitute?

When it happens – spills of petrol and turpentine substitute are usually accidental.

You will need

> fresh air
> 1 tbsp bicarb

Instinctively, the first thought is to throw the clothes into the washing machine, but unfortunately that may not rid the clothes of the smell and can make your washing machine smell, too.

The smelly clothes need to be dried or hung out in the open air so that the spirit or smoke can evaporate and disperse.

Once dried or left outside for a few hours, the clothes can be washed in the washing machine in the normal way – add a tablespoon of bicarb to the wash to neutralize any residual odour.

OIL AND FAT SPLASHES ON CLOTHING

Oil splashes and stains happen. Whether the splash is from cooking, make-up, sun cream or hair products, if not removed the stain will seem to get bigger every time you look at it. If dealt with straight away, it will not fix into the fabric.

How often do I need to remove oil and fat splashes?

As with any stain, quick action makes for a better result.

You will need

eco-friendly washing-up liquid/dish soap
1 tsp bicarb

Lay the garment out over an old towel, then drizzle over eco-friendly washing-up liquid. Sprinkle over the bicarb and work the two into a paste, massaging well into the stain, then leave for 15 minutes. Pop the garment into the washing machine and wash as normal.

An old, fixed oil stain can be removed in this way, but leave the paste on the garment for longer – say 30 minutes – before rinsing under the tap to examine whether the oil has been dissolved.

FRUIT AND VEG STAINS

Fruit and vegetable stains can seem to be the most stubborn and difficult to clean, but if dealt with quickly and correctly they need not be a lasting problem. Tablecloths, napkins, baby bibs, aprons, tea towels, children's clothing – so many items fall victim to fruit juices, pizza drips and tomato sauce.

How often do I need to remove fruit and veg stains?

As quickly as you can.

You will need

cold water
small bowl
6 tbsp white vinegar
eco-friendly washing-up liquid/dish soap
1 tbsp bicarb

First, do not toss the stained item into the washing machine – detergents and washing can actually fix the stain and it will be there forever.

Instead, prepare a bowl of cold water and add 6 tbsp white vinegar. Scrape away any surplus spill with a knife then pop the item into the water and leave to soak for several hours or overnight. The stain will disappear or pale in colour. A good rule of thumb is to use one part vinegar to three parts water in the bowl.

If there is still a hint of the stain, then rub over 1 tbsp bicarb with a squirt of washing-up liquid and massage in with the fingers – leave for 10 minutes, then pop into the washing machine.

FRUIT JUICE AND WINE STAINS

Berries, fruit juice and wine can be problem stains that will fix in fabric if not dealt with at the outset. This is a great little tip, especially handy for the wine drips or fruit spills that appear on your best white tablecloth.

How often do I need to treat fruit juice and wine stains?

As quickly as you can – I have only used this on fresh stains.

You will need

    kettle of boiling water
    bowl or colander

Lay the stained part of the item over an empty bowl or colander and place in the sink. Try to pull and hold the fabric fairly taut. Pour the boiling water over the stain in a thin, steady stream and see the stain disappear before your very eyes. This is a perfect fix for cottons, linens and robust natural materials. Not suitable for wool, silk or delicate fabrics – refer to the tip above using a cold water soak with vinegar.

AVOID A TRIP TO THE DRY-CLEANER!

Many garments have the dreaded 'dry-clean only' label, and while the finish and press are always professional and preferable, especially for garments such as coats, suits and jackets, how annoying that the whole garment might have to be dry-cleaned in order to remove a small make-up smudge around the collar or a grubby mark around the cuff!

Apart from the expense and inconvenience of having to take a trip to the dry-cleaner over one little mark, the chemical pollution created by many dry-cleaning substances is another reason to avoid using this cleaning method where possible.

I have a favourite black jacket, yet because the collar lies next to the skin, in no time at all there is a mark – either from make-up or perspiration – and it seems a nuisance to continually need to have the jacket dry-cleaned. I have found that a reusable cotton pad dampened with surgical spirit will clean the collar area quickly and effectively.

How often do I need to treat my dry-clean-only garments at home?

Whenever you want to remove an unsightly make-up mark from a collar or clean a grubby cuff.

You will need

  surgical spirit
  soft cotton pad (reusable make-up remover pad)

Lay the jacket or article out on a work surface and open up the collar or cuff to expose the line of the grubby mark. Dab with the spirit-soaked pad and see how quickly the mark lifts and immediately dries.

Another trip to the dry-cleaner avoided!

BODY ODOUR STAINS AND SMELLS

Have you ever washed items of clothing, particularly shirts and blouses made from artificial fibres, only to find when it comes to the ironing that there is a stale body odour and deodorant smell coming from the fabric? Even worse, you have had a suit or jacket dry-cleaned only to find there is stale body odour still present under the arms. Sometimes, perspiration and deodorant can leave a stain on shirts and blouses, too, making the fabric look faded or yellow.

How often do I need to treat body odour stains and smells?

Check your laundry before washing, and check the freshness of dry-clean-only garments.

You will need

warm water
2 tbsp bicarb
1–2 tbsp surgical spirit
small bowl
2–3 reusable cotton make-up
    remover pads

Bicarb is fantastic at dealing with both stains and odours. If the garments are washable, simply mix a very thin paste of 2 tbsp bicarb and warm water in a bowl, then take a reusable cotton pad well soaked in the thin paste and dab all over the stained or odorous area – don't be afraid to put plenty on. Leave for an hour, then pop the garment into the washing machine. Both the odour and stain will disappear.

It is a huge disappointment if body odour is still present following a professional clean. Or maybe it is that the garment, probably a jacket, is perfectly clean but just doesn't smell all that fresh. Another trip to the dry-cleaner needs to be avoided. Why waste more money and use more harmful chemicals when there is no need?

I tested this tip out on a black woollen dry-clean-only sweater. It was perfectly clean apart from perspiration odour under the arms. Rather than a trip to the dry-cleaner, I decided to rid the garment of the odour using the bicarb paste. Obviously I was mindful that I would probably clear the odour as I knew it worked well on fabrics before laundering, but washing was not an option as the garment would need to be dry-cleaned.

Taking two reusable cotton make-up remover pads well soaked in the thin bicarb paste, dab both of the underarm areas of the dry-clean-only garment. Give each underarm a good treatment and then leave the soaked pads on the garment overnight. The paste needs to remain damp, so it is a good idea to fold the garment up and place it in a plastic bag. The next day the pads should still be slightly damp. Remove them and leave the garment to dry naturally and completely. Any residual powder can be brushed off, and if there is the slightest hint of a white mark, a cotton pad dipped in surgical spirit and dabbed around the mark quickly removes that.

You may find yourself scanning every dry-clean-only garment in your wardrobe to do further work – I know I did. The same treatment on each worked a charm.

KITCHEN

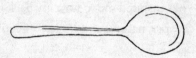

The kitchen is the heart of the home, and often it is the room that is used the most. Whenever anyone visits, the likelihood is they will sit in the kitchen and chat over a coffee. When friends and family come over for a meal, they tend to stand in the kitchen to chat. The kitchen produces the gorgeous homely smells of freshly baked bread, cake, soups and stews and everything that is comfy about home life.

It is no surprise, then, that as the kitchen is the busiest room it also produces some of the heftiest cleaning problems. Historically my kitchen was without doubt the room that commanded the largest variety of cleaning products – one for every eventuality. A shelf full of coloured plastic bottles promising the shiniest, cleanest, most sparkling results for my hob, oven, sink, fridge, drains, glass surfaces and dishwasher. I had wipes, sprays, liquids, gels and creams, and they all did a sterling job.

I can remember in my younger days trying to spread the cost of cleaning materials over several shops. They were so expensive, and could make a huge dent in my weekly shopping bill if I needed to stock up on everything at the same time.

I am delighted that my green and clean journey has relieved

me of the need to buy any of those products. Apart from their expense, their heavy use of harmful chemicals – clearly marked on the labels – has inspired me to turn my back on them and to favour much cheaper, natural and no less effective alternatives.

A PERFECT CUPPA!

I am a tea fan, and for us Brits tea is the perfect fit for so many occasions. If there's a crisis, a celebration, whether we're feeling too hot or too cold the answer is always, 'Let's put the kettle on.'

I always used teabags, and there are still those times when a teabag is much more convenient. Whether you brew in a cup or use bags or loose leaves in a pot, the tea tannin is unsightly and the stain can be problematic. I have to confess my solution always was to soak the teapot overnight in a chlorine bleach and water solution. Next morning the teapot was stain-free – a quick rinse and a wash in soapy water and off we go again.

Chlorine bleach is no longer allowed in my green and clean home. An alternative had to be found. If only I had applied this tip earlier. All those years of bleach use because I just didn't know! This natural, non-harmful way to clean tea and coffee stains from pots and mugs is quicker and not damaging to the environment, as chlorine bleach is.

How often do I need to treat the teapot or mugs?

Once a week, as a guide.

You will need

2 tbsp bicarb
rubber gloves
bottle brush

Wet the well-stained teapot, coffee pot or mug on the inside by running it under the tap. Pour out any water remaining. Sprinkle in a large tablespoon of bicarb, on with the rubber gloves and start work rubbing away at that tannin using your fingers to get into every nook and cranny. The tannin dissolves immediately and in seconds you will have a muddy-looking mess going on inside your pot or mug. A quick rinse with cold water, then in with the second tablespoon of bicarb, concentrating on any areas that have been missed. A bottle brush down the spout of the teapot will sort the most difficult to reach part of the task, then a final rinse under the tap and even the thickest brown tannin stain will have dissolved.

I have a teapot with a handy little basket that holds on to the leaves avoiding the need for a tea strainer when pouring.

This mesh basket gets very stained and although it is possible to remove the tannin stains using bicarb and a reusable scourer, a quicker method is half a teaspoon of green bleach into the teapot with the basket, fill with boiling water, leave it standing in the sink and in just 30 minutes all will be clean without effort.

Teabags are convenient, suitable for a one-mug brew and can easily be disposed of – but can they? Therein lies the problem, because many teabags contain plastic and there is even a suggestion that some of that plastic may leak out into the tea. Apart from all of that is the taste. I can definitely tell the difference between a cup of tea made with loose leaves and one made from a teabag – so I'm a loose leaf lady, myself!

DISHWASHER DETERGENT AND RINSE AID

This tip nearly didn't make it into the book, even though it was one of the first green alternatives I started working on several years ago. The dishwasher ended up being my Achilles heel! There are sites online promising the best home-made potions and tablets, and perfect results every time. Many sites and videos have had thousands and thousands of views, which gave me hope of success, but every single one let me down.

How many times I have thought something would work only to find, after two or three wash cycles, the cups are staining, glasses are cloudy or there are grains of food left on the plates! Trust me, I tried every possible concoction, I trialled them so many times and nearly gave up. I even read around the use of Epsom salts and their efficiency as a dishwasher detergent. Brilliant, I thought. Epsom salts purchased, loaded into the dishwasher, only to find that not only were the pots and glasses covered in a thick white film, but the inside of the dishwasher was, too. It took several cycles before the stains dissolved.

Supermarket own-brand dishwasher tablets cost about a third of the price of their eco-friendly alternatives. I had to try to sort it myself. This recipe will cost no more than the supermarket own brands, is safe for the environment and will clean plates and shine glasses. However, it isn't suitable for absolutely all machine types, especially in hard water areas, so do check the results and your machine carefully after first use. If this detergent doesn't work for you, don't discard it. Add 1–2 tbsp to your whites laundry wash cycle.

Dishwasher tablets have a long and complex list of toxic chemicals which are bad for the environment and many are sealed in their own single-use plastic cover, which, we are told, dissolves – but isn't this just more plastic being literally washed down the drain?

If you are becoming a dedicated green cleaner, then you will recognize that the rinse aid recipe is similar to my recipe for laundry fabric conditioner. It does the same job, really – the vinegar softens the water for the final rinse and prevents any limescale build-up on glassware. I have added a little surgical spirit (rubbing alcohol), which cleans, is quick-drying and eliminates streaks or water marks. Vegetable glycerine is a natural stain solvent, and the lemon essential oil will get rid of any remaining grease and deodorizes, too.

When it comes to rinse aid, there is information stating that vinegar should not be used in the rinse aid compartment of the dishwasher as it can corrode parts. I then went on to further read that rinse aid can contain vinegar and surgical spirit anyway! I will leave it up to you to decide, only to say that this combo works for me. Many dishwashers use about 1 tbsp rinse aid per cycle, so rather than leave it standing in the dispenser, I add it at the same time I add the detergent every time the dishwasher is used. In this way, I consider that I am minimizing the risk (if there is one) of vinegar corrosion.

Many machines, particularly in Europe are fitted with a built-in water softener that has to be topped up with very coarse sodium chloride (salt). There will be a special compartment inside the dishwasher, often at the base, where the salt is to be added when the machine sensor alerts a top-up is needed – usually about once a month. If the dishwasher has run out of salt, limescale deposits can appear, particularly on glassware, making them look dull or cloudy. However, if you run out don't be tempted to use table salt as an alternative as it is much finer and can block and cause damage to your dishwasher. Dishwasher salt granules are large, ensuring the salt dissolves slowly without blocking the softener unit.

How often do I use the clean and green dishwasher detergent and rinse aid?

Each time you put the dishwasher through a cycle. The following makes sufficient detergent for 25 washes.

You will need

DETERGENT

100g green bleach

300g washing soda

100g bicarb

500g jar

20g measuring spoon

RINSE AID

200ml white vinegar

10ml surgical spirit

15ml vegetable glycerine

20 drops organic lemon essential oil

small funnel

Detergent

Make up a jar of detergent by combining the green bleach, washing soda and bicarb in a jar, give it a good stir and find a spoon that measures exactly 20g to keep in the jar. I have a plastic medicine spoon that just happens to be an exact measure. Use an eco, full wash cycle rather than a quickie wash, and when the plates are heavily soiled and the dishwasher is really full, run a rinse cycle first. As a routine, if there are plates in the dishwasher but it's not yet full, I run the rinse cycle most days. Mine is just 15 minutes and not only does it prevent food drying on really hard it also prevents any odour.

Use a 20g measure of the detergent in each cycle and try to get into the habit of giving the contents of your jar a stir before using. The green bleach tends to find its way to the top of the jar, so a stir every time it is used will ensure a well-combined mix.

Rinse Aid

Make up a bottle of the rinse aid by funnelling each of the liquids into your container and use 1 tbsp per cycle, measuring it into the rinse aid compartment at the same time as you load the detergent.

DISHWASHER CLEAN AND FRESHEN UP!

Those of us with a dishwasher probably switch it on every other day – I do, at any rate. From time to time, particularly if it hasn't been checked and cleaned, it can become odorous, and you may notice food particles left in the bottom of cups or sticking to cutlery. These are the signs that you need to take some action.

When engaging in my now regular pastime of perusing the supermarket cleaning product shelves, I have noted a number of proprietary cleaners specifically for the dishwasher. These can be quite pricey, the most expensive I found (at around £10) promising a full dishwasher maintenance wash and new life for an old dishwasher! Hefty chemical clean, hefty price and in my opinion, a task that can be carried out cheaply, naturally and effectively with a little thought.

How often do I need to clean and freshen up the dishwasher?

I give my dishwasher a clean about once a month (maybe two!), and as a one-off always before I go on holiday.

You will need

  eco-friendly washing-up liquid/dish soap
  3–4 spent lemon halves or 4 tbsp white vinegar
  old toothbrush

The first task is to remove the bottom drawer of the machine so that the filter can be accessed easily. The filter in my machine is found underneath a stainless steel removable plate containing drainage holes, and sits inside a removable plastic cup. Remove the plate, the cup and the filter. You may be surprised at the state of your filter if you have not removed this before. Peas in particular tend to get wedged in there, as do other kinds of unrecognizable food debris. There will also be a greasy feel to the filter.

Remove any solid matter and pop it in the bin (not down the sink), then, under a running tap, rinse away as much of the debris as you can.

Have a bowl of hot water and eco-friendly washing-up liquid ready: together this solution will break down any remaining grease and grime. Use an old toothbrush and scourer to get into all the filter parts. When the filter is clean, rinse it under cold water and pop it back into the machine.

It is now necessary to run the machine on a hot cycle while

empty. If you have some spent lemon halves to hand, then pop them onto the top shelf of the dishwasher, making sure you have removed any pips. Alternatively, put the lemon halves into a little string bag to catch any errant pips. (If there are pips left they can become a problem if they clog your filter.)

If you don't have lemons, then pour 4 tbsp white vinegar into the machine before you switch it on.

The empty wash plus the acid from the lemons or the vinegar will clean, shine, deodorize and dissolve any grease in the dishwasher. After the wash remove the lemons and discard. Your machine will be shiny, fresh and clean.

CLEAN OVEN SHELVES WHILE YOU SLEEP

Even the cleanest cook will encounter burnt-on deposits, spills and splashes to the oven shelves. I have memories of tirelessly standing with a pad of wire wool scrubbing away at each metal piece, splashing brown greasy marks onto the kitchen window, sink and floor. The metal shelves were a dread. Then I discovered branded products that did the job effortlessly. I'd pop the whole lot into a huge bag, pour in the caustic gel and everything cleaned up like magic.

I didn't quite understand that the sodium hydroxide (caustic soda) that makes up the main part of many oven cleaners was so very harmful. I remember using a pastry brush to get into the difficult parts of the oven, only to find the bristles had dissolved away after just a few minutes. Warnings were given about burns to skin, a threat to eyes, nose, throat and respiratory airways.

I needed an effortless clean with no potential hazards to health.

How often do I need to clean the oven shelves?

This natural method of cleaning your stainless steel oven shelves is so effortless, and can be done as and when required – in fact, you will enjoy it!

You will need

> 2–3 cups washing soda
> hot water
> sink or plastic box large enough to hold your oven shelves

In a sink large enough to take your oven shelves, or a sturdy plastic box, measure 2–3 cups of washing soda. If your shelves are really grubby, make a double concentrate and use 4–6 cups. Pour in sufficient boiling water to cover your shelves. If you do two shelves your water needs to be about 3 inches (7cm) deep.

Pop your metal shelves into the hot solution making sure they are submerged and leave them overnight.

I have found that if the shelves are hot when submerged the cleaning is quicker and more effective, but you may want to avoid shelves being too hot if you are using a plastic box.

The next day lift your shelves out of the brown, muddy water and wipe clean – that's it.

You can pour the water down the drain knowing no harm is being done.

NOTE: If your oven shelves have been sprayed or coated with 'self-clean' substances, do not use this method. The chemical coating can be damaged by soaking. This method is not suitable for aluminium trays or shelves. Aluminium can be cleaned using bicarb or washing soda, but long soaks cause oxidization.

USE GRASS TO CLEAN OVEN AND BARBECUE RACKS

Want to clean your oven shelves or barbecue racks? Step out onto the lawn!

This is a great way to clean large metal racks from barbecues and ovens. It works all year round, but I have found that it is in the spring and early summer months, when the grass is growing well and is green and vibrant, that the best results are achieved.

Simply place your grubby shelf or rack onto the grass. I have found this method works best if the oven shelf is just slightly warm and the grass is long and slightly damp. Even better, if the grass has just been mowed, bury the shelf in the fresh clippings. Leave the shelves for 24 hours, then wipe clean.

If your rack is grubby on both sides it may take a day longer – just flip it over after 24 hours and leave for another day. Wipe clean with a dry cloth.

Try it for the entertainment value after your summer barbecue!

THOROUGH, EFFECTIVE OVEN CLEAN WITHOUT HARMFUL CHEMICALS

Deep cleaning the oven! Anyone like doing it? Have to admit, not my favourite cleaning task, but working with a greasy, smelly oven feels just wrong.

For many years I bought a proprietary cleaner for my oven: a caustic chemical clean, left on overnight. The warnings to not inhale the fumes, to wear rubber gloves and dispose of the hazardous waste carefully is now a thing of the past. Apart from being completely natural and non-hazardous, this cleaning method is not expensive. A thorough clean of your oven, and at minimum cost!

How often do I need to deep clean the oven?

Twice a year.

You will need

60ml warm water
150g bicarb
½ tsp xanthan gum (optional)
small bowl and spoon
rubber gloves
pastry brush
fine wire wool

plastic bench scraper
cloths

Start by boiling a kettle of water.

Remove the metal shelves, side runners and back plate – in fact all removable items – and carry out a soak in washing soda as described for oven shelves in the previous tip (see pages 85–6).

Use either the grill pan or a large roasting tin, and place it in the bottom of the oven. Switch the oven on to 100°C. Once the oven has reached temperature, open the door and pour a full kettle of boiling water into the grill pan or roasting tin. Close the oven door, switch off the oven and leave for 20 minutes.

The heat and the steam will soften the baked-on splashes and drips which are covering your oven walls and base.

In the meantime, mix a paste. Measure the bicarb into a bowl and add the xanthan gum (if using), then add the warm water little by little until you have a thick but runny paste. If you don't have xanthan gum, don't worry, but it does help to make the paste easier to brush on. It is used in gluten-free bakes to improve the consistency of gluten-free flour and to give it a bit of stretch.

Return to the oven. You will see that the glass door has steamed up and the oven sides are wet. Remove the roasting tin or grill pan and carefully discard the hot water.

To make your oven easier to work on, unhinge the door, if you can. If not, you will need to reach into the back of the oven. On with the rubber gloves, and start to apply the bicarb paste all over the oven, dabbing with the pastry brush until every inch is covered.

Leave for 20–30 minutes, then carry out a test. Use your piece of fine wire wool to rub in circular motions and see the baked-on deposits lift. If your oven is really grubby you may need to leave the paste on longer, though I find it better and easier to work with the paste before it has completely dried.

Continue working until the oven is clean. Using a bench scraper, collect the dirty bicarb paste, scrape it into a bowl and discard.

Then take a bowl of clean hot soapy water (use eco-friendly washing-up liquid) and a cloth and clean up the remainder of the paste. Any bits that have been missed can be rubbed with the wire wool. Your oven is sparkling – no fumes, no harmful chemicals and at minimal cost.

If you have been able to remove your oven door, it is easy to clean on a work surface using the same bicarb paste. If you have cooking spills between the glass, it is often possible to separate the glass panels and clean in between. Check the instruction booklet that came with the oven, or look up the make and model online. Mine is very simple to remove. Again, use the bicarb paste, leave on then gently rub off with either a sponge or fine wire wool.

There is something very satisfying about a clean oven!

NOTE: If your oven has 'self-clean' sides or floor, do not use this method. The 'self-clean' coating may be damaged by using the bicarb paste.

Once clean, it is quite easy to keep the oven looking good for many months if you get into the habit of doing the following.

1 After every time I use the oven, I wipe the inside of the glass door with a clean, damp cloth while the oven is still warm. You will be surprised – just baking a loaf of bread, which you may consider a clean use of the oven, will leave a brown film on the glass door. Fat splashes will just wipe off if cleaned every time the oven is used. Just do not allow them to bake on.

2 A second tip is to pop the oven shelves out on the lawn before you go to bed at the first sign of burnt-on deposits (see page 87). They will self-clean. Alternatively, if you do not have a green space, then an overnight soak as described previously (see pages 85–6) is completely effortless but keeps your oven more than acceptable.

INDUCTION, GAS OR CERAMIC HOB CLEANER

I have a very dated induction hob and it still sparkles like new. I was told when I bought it that I needed to use the proprietary cleaner that was recommended with the appliance. This is so often the case – we are advised to only use certain branded products. Of course we are! Then I realized this particular cleaner was so chemical-heavy, quite expensive and came well packaged in so many layers of plastic that I decided to have a go using my favourite ingredients.

How often do I need to clean the induction hob?

Thorough clean once every three to six months. Daily wipe and shine.

You will need

FOR A THOROUGH CLEAN
bowl of warm water with a squirt of eco-friendly washing-up
    liquid/dish soap
3–4 tbsp bicarb
warm water
white vinegar (better in a spray bottle)
dishcloth
rubber gloves
soft polishing cloth

FOR A DAILY SHINE AND POLISH
white vinegar in a spray bottle
clean, damp cloth
soft polishing cloth

Thorough clean

If your hob has knobs they will probably just pull off, leaving a hole and metal post underneath. Remove the knobs and wash separately in warm soapy water. Removing the knobs enables every part of the hob to be cleaned of greasy smears and splashes – almost impossible if knobs are present. Many modern hobs I see don't have control knobs – everything is touch control. Even better!

Wipe over the cold hob with a clean, damp cloth ensuring the whole of the surface is quite damp. Sprinkle over the bicarb. Using a gloved hand and more warm water as necessary (use the cloth to drip over extra water as needed), mix the bicarb and warm water together in small circular movements until it has been worked into a thin paste. Continue to massage the paste into the hob for maybe 2–3 minutes. Get the music on, dance and enjoy yourself. You can actually feel rough, greasy areas underneath your fingers becoming smooth as the bicarb does its work and the grease has to give way under its influence.

Leave the paste in place for 30 minutes, then use a bowl of warm soapy water and a cloth to remove the paste. Rinse the cloth well between each wipe.

The hob will be free from any marks and stains.

Once the hob is cleared of the bicarb paste and is pristine and gorgeous, give it a final shine and polish. A spray over with white vinegar and a massage around with gloved hands as before, then wipe off. Finally shine the hob up using a soft, dry polishing cloth.

If necessary, after soaking the knobs in soapy water, use a damp cloth dipped in a little bicarb to remove any stubborn stains. Once thoroughly dried, the knobs can then be popped back into their rightful places.

Daily shine and polish

To keep your induction hob always looking pristine, try to get into the habit of a quick clean after each use. Once cooled down, wipe with a soft, wet dishcloth, spray with white vinegar, wipe and buff dry with a dry cloth – that will be all it needs.

Gas hobs and stainless steel will clean up in exactly the same way. Badly burnt-on deposits can be cleaned using the paste as above. Remove the burners and pop them into hot water, then I clean these with fine wire wool dipped in dry bicarb.

Be careful when applying the bicarb paste to avoid obstructing or clogging up the burners themselves. Stainless steel hobs are easy to keep clean – a wipe over with a damp cloth when cool, followed by a spray of all-purpose cleaner and a buff with a soft cloth to shine and polish is often all that is required.

MICROWAVE CLEANING

The microwave oven is a handy tool for reheating, defrosting, some cooking, and is great at rushing things along. I freshen, boil and whiten dishcloths in mine, too (see pages 55–7).

It is a kitchen appliance that can be easily overlooked when it comes to cleaning, but splashes do occur and can fix onto the walls and roof of the microwave. The turntable, too, can get grubby.

How often do I need to clean the microwave?

Once every three months.

You will need

half a used lemon
hot water to cover the
    lemon
bowl of warm water with
    a squirt of eco-friendly
    washing-up liquid/dish
    soap
small microwave-proof bowl
dishcloth

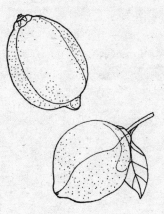

A quick and effective way to clean the microwave is to pop half a used lemon in a small microwave-proof bowl, cover the lemon with recently boiled water or hot water from the tap and put the microwave on full power for 1½–2 minutes or until you see the water bubble.

Once the microwave has pinged, leave for 2 minutes then open the door, remove the bowl and lemon (be careful – it will be hot), then use a wrung-out cloth that has been dipped in warm water and eco-friendly washing-up liquid to wipe the inside of the microwave. The steam softens any cooked-on splashes and the lemon freshens up the unit.

DEODORIZE, SANITIZE AND TREAT WOODEN SPOONS AND BOARDS

I love my collection of wooden spoons, and one or two I have had for forty years or more. Looked after correctly, your wooden utensils will last a lifetime.

Mine are very well used, and I tend to consider my wooden utensils as heirlooms – unlike their throwaway plastic equivalents.

To keep them looking good, clean and to prevent cracking, the spoons need attention. Using a wooden spoon to stir onions can result in it absorbing the odour. Although I tend to use the same spoon for onions, thereby limiting the problem, from time to time the smell still needs to be eradicated.

How often do I need to deodorize, sanitize and treat wooden spoons?

Routinely maybe once a month, or when you detect a smelly spoon.

You will need

TO DEODORIZE
80–100ml white vinegar
water

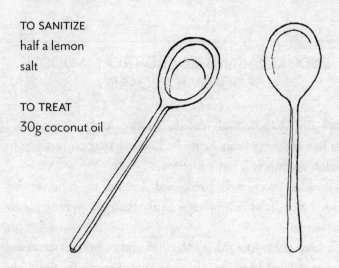

TO SANITIZE
half a lemon
salt

TO TREAT
30g coconut oil

To neutralize wooden spoon odours

I use a mug or a vessel large enough to take the spoon. Pour over enough white vinegar to come about a third of the way up the spoon, then top up with water. The liquid needs to come to the level where the handle starts – about 3 inches (7cm) deep. Leave for an hour.

After the soak the spoon can then be hand-washed in warm soapy water.

When it comes to washing wooden spoons, the golden rule is to never put them in the dishwasher. The machine is too severe, and eventually your spoons will dry out and crack lengthways.

To sanitize and treat wooden utensils

Rub the lemon half over both sides of the spoon, then sprinkle with a little table salt and use your fingers to massage the spoon. Rinse in warm soapy water – just eco-friendly washing-up liquid – dry with a clean tea towel then stand the spoons, handle side down, in a mug or jug.

Allow to air-dry thoroughly.

Never be tempted to put damp wooden spoons into a cutlery drawer, as mould could start to grow on them. I keep my wooden utensils handle side down in a wide pot – air circulates around them all of the time, ensuring there is no mould or odour building up.

To treat and prolong the life of wooden utensils and chopping boards, they need a feed from time to time. Coconut oil will gently moisturize the wood, preventing it from drying out and cracking. I like to warm my jar of coconut oil slightly by leaving it either on a sunny windowsill or a radiator for half an hour so that it is soft and creamy.

Apply with the finger and massage onto the dried spoons and see how gorgeous, rich and wholesome they look. Leave for 15 minutes to allow it to soak in then polish with a dry cloth. It's a pleasure keeping my spoons out in the kitchen – I just love to look at them.

FRESHEN SMELLY CHOPPING BOARDS

There are some fantastic chopping boards on the market – colour-coded and modern, or you may have favourite wooden boards. I have a set of the colourful ones and I love them, but my wooden ones are my favourites. I suppose the sentiment is the same between wooden spoons and plastic spatulas – which one would you want as an heirloom?

Whichever boards you have, what happens when you reach for the green 'fruit and veggie' board and it smells odorous? You need it to chop up the fruit for your fruit salad, but find it smells strongly of onions from the last time you used it.

How often do I need to clean the chopping board?

After every use.

You will need

half a lemon
table salt

Try to get into the habit of wiping the board down with half a lemon or a squirt of 'jiffy' lemon juice after chopping garlic or onions. The lemon will neutralize the smells and your board will be fine to use every time.

If onion and garlic are left to impregnate the board it can be very difficult to eradicate, but if you find the lemon hasn't quite cut through the odour, then sprinkle over a tablespoon of table salt, rub it in and leave for 15 minutes. Then use half a lemon, rubbing it over the salt in small circular movements. The salt and lemon juice together will bleach the board clean and at the same time neutralize any lingering smell.

RECYCLING GLASS JARS WITHOUT A VINEGAR SMELL

As I work at phasing out single-use plastic in my home – and have not been using cling film for some years – I have found that glass jars with screw-top lids are perfect for storing food in the fridge. Unused egg whites, egg yolks, grated cheese, leftovers of all kinds keep perfectly fresh in clean, airtight glass jars.

But how often have you taken a recycled and clean glass jar, unscrewed the lid and had to step back when the old strong vinegar smell hits you? I make my own jams and pickles, and a smelly pickle jar will not work well with my fresh, fruity strawberry jam. Jars and lids with a strong vinegar odour will not upcycle well in their present state.

How often do I need to deodorize recycled glass jars?

Whenever you detect a smelly jar or lid.

You will need

2 tsp bicarb
1 tsp warm water

If, after a thorough wash in warm soapy water, the jar still has a vinegar odour, then while the jar is still wet on the inside, sprinkle in 1–2 tsp bicarb. Add a teaspoon of warm water to the powder to make a paste and, using your fingers (or even a piece of scrunched-up newspaper if the jar has a narrow neck), simply work your way around the jar then leave for 15 minutes with the paper still inside, if using. Remove the paper, rinse out the jar and have a sniff. Your jar will be fresh and odour-free.

Lids of jars can take on odour, too, and sometimes the seal around the top can discolour. Sprinkle about a teaspoon of bicarb into the seal and rim of a slightly dampened lid and rub, then leave for 10–15 minutes. Rinse and dry and the lid is odour-free.

RAINWATER FOR JAR ODOURS

Leaving a smelly jar and lid outside in the rain for a day or two will neutralize odours. Don't forget about it, though! I did, then found it months later full of water, a few leaves and sticks. I brought it inside, gave it a good wash and it is back in circulation.

Unscrew the lid, pop the lid and jar outside in the rain for a day. Next day wash them in warm soapy water, dry and the pungent smell will have gone.

STICKY LABEL REMOVER

I now reuse glass jars for all kinds of things. The obvious being jams, preserves and pickles. There will also be those pretty jars and bottles that have spray attachments, pump dispensers and attractive, colourful screw-top lids. There are so many recipes in this book that call for recycled glass containers, including lip balm and hand sanitizer. I have also bought my own new glass bottles for polish, floor cleaner, fabric softener, all-purpose cleaner – the list goes on.

All bottles and jars need to be labelled but, when that bottle, jar or container is empty, washed out and put back into circulation, how annoying to find that even after a soak and a cycle in the dishwasher there are still cloudy, sticky remains from the previous label.

I confess to having bought solvents and used nail varnish remover in an attempt to return my jars to their previous sparkly, non-sticky glory – until I tried this!

How often do I need to remove sticky labels from jars?

Whenever you want to upcycle a favourite jar but not the sticky label.

You will need

1 tbsp vegetable oil (spray oil works too)
1 tbsp bicarb
soft cloth

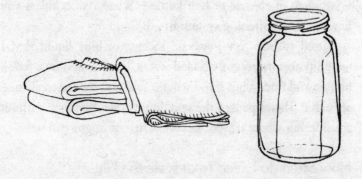

Take a soft cloth, dip it into a little vegetable oil and dab it onto the sticky patch. Then take the same cloth and dab on the bicarb. Leave for 15 minutes then wipe away any label remnants and sticky residue. If you have a bottle of spray oil even easier. Spray oil onto the label, sprinkle over the bicarb and massage in with your fingers. Leave for 15 minutes then wipe off with a cloth.

KETTLE DESCALE

If you live in a hard water area, limescale build-up in your kettle – whether an electric or hob kettle – is inevitable, unless you have a water-softening system fitted.

I used to buy very powerful sachets of blue liquid that I would pour into recently boiled water. There would be a fizz, a bubble and fumes, but it did what it said and the limescale disappeared. Then I poured the said liquid down the drain without considering where it went next or where it might end up!

How often do I need to descale the kettle?

Clean your badly scaled kettle, then do a maintenance descale once a month.

You will need

    80g citric acid for a thorough clean
    1–2 lemons for regular maintenance

It is possible to quickly and effectively descale a kettle naturally, without fumes and without damaging our water system. If, like me, you tend to leave the kettle longer than you intended before descaling, then an initial super-clean is required. Half fill your kettle with water and boil. Unplug it, if electric, and stand the kettle in the empty sink (the citric acid will cause the water to bubble up). Add 80g citric acid and leave for half an hour. The limescale will dissolve. Pour away the liquid, knowing that the citric acid joining the waterways is having no adverse effects.

Before pouring away the citric acid solution, I always tip my kettle on its side so that the water fills and dissolves any limescale build-up in the spout. Wedge the underside of the kettle with a cloth to keep it in a tipping position.

A kettle free of limescale will use less energy to boil, too, so it is important to try to keep the limescale at bay. Citric acid (derived from citrus fruits) and acetic acid (from vinegar) will both dissolve limescale. I choose citric acid because there is no residual smell. Who wants the kitchen smelling of vinegar while the kettle descales?

I now have a habit that if I have used lemons for baking or cooking, I drop them into the kettle before I go to bed, bring it to the boil and leave them there overnight. The next day I pour away the water, discard the lemons and the kettle is kept bright, shiny and efficient.

The spout of the kettle can look unsightly as limescale builds up there too. Even after a thorough clean and descale of the whole of the vessel, how do you get to the tip of the spout? Pop a lemon half onto the spout (I also lay a sliver down the funnel part) at bedtime and remove the next morning. Limescale dissolved!

ALL-PURPOSE CLEANER FOR THE KITCHEN AND BATHROOM

When I came up with this cleaner I decided it would be perfect for wiping down my kitchen worktops, cupboards and shelves. The vinegar helps to kill germs and cuts through any grease, grime and limescale, and the surgical spirit also kills germs, adds a super-fresh clean smell and helps the spray evaporate and shine up easily. Adding a few drops of essential oil gives a little perfume. The essential oil has its own antiseptic and cleaning properties, too. The water is simply a diluent – it makes the cleaner go further by diluting the ingredients.

How often do I need to use all-purpose cleaner?

This cleaner does what it says – I use it all around the home on most days.

You will need

60ml white vinegar
150ml water
40ml surgical spirit
20 drops organic essential oil
    (lemon and eucalyptus are my
    favourites)
300ml glass bottle with spray
    attachment

Easy to make: simply place the measured ingredients into a glass spray bottle, give it a shake and you are ready to go. Label the bottle. It is a good idea to write a second label with the ingredients and stick it to the back of the bottle (or use glass paint for a permanent fix), so that when you are ready for a refill it is quick and easy to do.

This cleaner is brilliant! I use it to clean mirrors, tiles and glass – a quick spray then polish with a clean, dry polishing cloth.

I use it to clean my shower screen, wash-hand basin and bath. It smells great, does the job and I am saved from having to buy a whole range of plastic-packaged cleaning products – no bathroom cleaner, no kitchen cleaner, no tile cleaner, no glass cleaner and no harmful chemicals, no extra packaging and no plastic. Cheap to make, too – I am saving a fortune!

KITCHEN TAPS: THE SPOUTS HAVE
A LIMESCALE CRUST

Limescale deposits can form a crust around the tap spout. I have a mixer tap, and at one time it got so bad the water flow was affected. The water appeared to come out of the tap at a lopsided angle!

I used to buy proprietary limescale removers, but trying to treat the underside of a tap spout was nearly impossible, other than standing for twelve hours with limescale remover in a cup holding it over the underside of the tap!

How often do I need to descale the kitchen taps?

Once every three months if you live in a hard water area, like me.

You will need

1 lemon – even better, use a spent lemon that has already been used for its zest and juice

Nature provides us with the perfect vessel – a lemon half. A spent lemon half stuck onto the end of a tap before you go to bed, maybe secured with an elastic band, will do the job perfectly and cheaply without the need for any packaged preparations. The next day remove the lemon halves, wipe the ends of your taps with a damp cloth and see them shine.

KITCHEN SINK CLEANING

I have a huge confession to make! My daily routine at the kitchen sink used to be a squirt of chlorine bleach before I went to bed, a swirl around with a long-handled brush, a further squirt down the plughole – job done.

Two problems occurred: first, I destroyed the composite finish of my white ceramic sink. After repeated use of the chlorine, pitted areas appeared – the surface had corroded. Secondly, I was, every day without fail, adding to the pollutants being poured into our waterways.

One new sink and a heightened awareness later, I turned to straightforward bicarb as it will not corrode my sink in the way that chlorine bleach did.

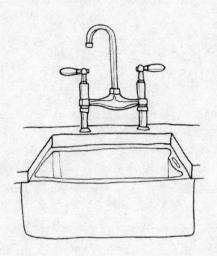

How often do I need to clean the kitchen sink?

I clean my kitchen sink every day – it takes less than 5 minutes.

You will need

1 tbsp bicarb
soft cloth

A tablespoon of bicarb sprinkled around the bowl and a soft cloth will quickly and effectively remove any stains. A quick rinse, and it is as white as new. Works really well on stainless steel, too.

KITCHEN SINK DRAIN

If you drink tea or coffee, pouring the leftovers down the sink will often result in brown, unsightly stains around the plug and down the waste. Worst-case scenario is unpleasant smells coming from the kitchen sink.

Never poke food debris down the plug – remove it and put it in the bin. Food lodged in the waste pipe will rot and smell.

How often do I need to clean the kitchen sink drain?

I refresh the kitchen drain once a week.

You will need

125g washing soda
long-handled sink brush

Keeping your kitchen sink and drain looking and smelling gorgeous is simple, clean and green. After your daily sink clean, measure out 125g of washing soda and pour it into the plughole. It will sit there in a lump. Leave it and go to bed or do it before you go out – or at least at a time when you will not need your sink. Leave it for a couple of hours as a minimum.

The next day, or when you come home, take a long-handled sink brush and scrub away at the plug. The metal will shine up like new, any tea or coffee stains will have been cleaned away and the waste pipe will be clean and fresh.

A rinse from the tap, and your sink is beautiful.

DON'T FORGET THE OVERFLOW

A daily sink clean with bicarb is now part of my everyday routine, plus washing soda for the drain and all is done – but is it?

All sinks are fitted with an overflow which, thankfully, is seldom needed. Only if the tap is left on and the sink is in danger of overflowing do we ever give it a passing thought. I urge you to give it a spray and a scrub with a bottle brush – if it is anything like mine, there is a crust of black mould lingering in there. It makes sense, really – mould loves dark, damp conditions and will happily grow if not disturbed, cleaned and treated.

How often do I need to clean the sink overflow?

Try to incorporate an overflow clean into your daily sink clean, or at least once a month.

You will need

spray bottle of all-purpose cleaner (see pages 108–9)
small bottle brush

Spray the all-purpose cleaner directly into the overflow – twist the nozzle on your bottle from fine spray to 'stream' and the liquid will get straight to the spot. Leave for a minute or two, then in with your baby bottle brush. Black mould will be released. Continue with the brush, spraying the cleaner directly onto it until eventually the brush comes out clean.

The vinegar in the spray will help kill mould spores, the surgical spirit will help to clean germs, and the essential oil with its own antiseptic properties will leave your sink and overflow smelling clean and fresh.

I HAVE RUST MARKS IN MY KITCHEN SINK!

I have an old and beautiful Belfast sink which, because of its size, is perfect for soaking oven shelves and parts for overnight cleaning. Any bare, untreated metal parts can leave a rust stain which can be shocking at first sight. Even a small screw or paper clip dropped into a sink and not removed immediately can cause a stubborn rust stain. No worries, though – they can be treated easily without having to resort to the purchase of branded chemical products.

How often do I need to clean rust marks in the sink?

Treat rust marks as soon as they appear.

You will need

- lemon juice ('jiffy' lemon juice will do)
- table salt

Apply a squirt of lemon juice followed by a sprinkle of table salt. Leave for at least an hour, or even better overnight. The next day no abrasives will be required – just a wipe with a damp cloth.

What if I told you I cleaned my rusty forty-year-old bike with lemon juice, salt and wire wool? This natural combo can take on any rust job.

FRIDGE CLEANING

Whether you have a super-modern fridge that defrosts itself or an old one that has to be turned off at the mains and defrosted, they all need to be cleaned regularly to keep them efficient and free of germs and bacteria.

A weekly check over of your fridge and its contents is always a good idea. Have a look at your 'use by' dates, make sure food is securely wrapped and that there have been no spills or leaks. Going over the shelves with a clean cloth and warm soapy water and then rearranging the contents is useful and acts as an aide-memoire if you are putting together your weekly shopping list.

How often do I need to clean the fridge?

Tidy and wipe down the fridge once a week. A thorough clean maybe every six months.

You will need

squirt of eco-friendly washing-up liquid in a bowl of warm water
2 tbsp bicarb
2 tbsp lemon juice
soft cloths

Giving your fridge a weekly check over and a quick clean is easier to do when you are ready to do a shop and there is not much to clear out. Use a squeezed-out, clean dishcloth to quickly wipe down the sides and bottom of the fridge as well as the shelves. If there are any stains left from bottles or spills, then dipping the cloth in a little bicarb will lift off even the most stubborn marks. If there is a plunger fitted at the back of the fridge above the drainage hole, check to make sure it is clean and that the drainage hole is not blocked.

A squirt of lemon juice to your clean, wrung-out cloth and a final wipe around, including the door seals, will help to kill any bacteria or potential mould or mildew problems that may be lurking and will leave a fresh 'just cleaned' smell, too.

Every six months or so (Christmastime and before going away on a summer holiday), I try to carry out a more thorough clean of the fridge. I take out all of the food, every bottle and jar. I take out the shelves and storage boxes and give everything a thorough wash in soapy water. I wipe down the sides and bottom of the fridge.

I adopted this 'deep clean' routine following a time when I walked into the kitchen to find a pool of water on the kitchen floor. I couldn't quite work it out. When I opened the fridge door, the back wall was completely frozen. The fridge was quite new at the time – I had no idea what was going on.

I have written this up as an alert in case it happens to you. I emptied the fridge of all the food, wiped down the shelves but then noticed that the drainage hole at the back of the fridge was black! Yes – I had ignored the fundamental part of any fridge clean.

Imagine what can find itself flowing into that drainage hole. A parsley leaf may have stuck onto the back wall of your fridge, or maybe a small piece of cheese, a splodge of cream or spill of milk. The automatic defrost would then carry that piece of food debris all the way down to the draining channel and onward into the drainage hole where it will rot, bung up the hole and cause the fridge to malfunction.

To avoid this, first take out the plastic plunger. This plunger is installed so that the drainage hole is always kept open and free-flowing, allowing the distilling water to drain away easily and efficiently. My plunger was unsightly and was immediately washed and, when I looked closely, the drainage hole was even worse.

Secondly, take a cloth. I used a metal skewer inside the cloth so that I could get right down that drainage hole, turning and cleaning repeatedly until the hole was clean and the cloth black! I replaced the plunger, and the pool of water and frozen fridge problem has never returned.

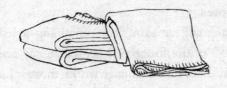

FRIDGE ODOURS

There are times when a strong odour is left in the fridge long after the offending food item has been removed. I recall leaving half a cut onion uncovered in the fridge and the smell lingered even though the onion was taken out.

How often do I need to deal with fridge odours?

Whenever an unpleasant residual odour is detected.

You will need

2–3 tbsp lemon juice
small ramekin dish
small piece of sponge to fit the dish

Simply place the sponge into the ramekin dish and pour the lemon juice over.

Leaving a small ramekin dish containing a lemon-juice-soaked sponge in the fridge will neutralize any residual food odour quickly. Bottled lemon juice works, though I have found fresh lemon juice to be more effective. I freeze any surplus lemon juice into ice cube trays, then reach for a cube when I need it for any of my cleaning recipes.

REMOVING MOULD AND MILDEW
FROM FRIDGE SEALS

The fungus that causes mould thrives in cold, dark and damp conditions. Coupled with bacteria and food debris, this means the average household fridge can be a breeding ground for germs, mould and mildew.

I have to confess, I allowed my fridge seals to become dotted with black mould. It is unsightly and unhealthy. If like me your first thought is to reach for a spray bottle of kitchen cleaner, mould or mildew treatment – stop! I realized I was probably going to be spraying all sorts of harmful chemicals into the one vessel where I stored the majority of my food!

I had to think again, and once on my clean and green journey I realized there were natural alternatives that could do a perfect job.

How often do I need to clean the fridge seals?

Once cleaned, your fridge seals will need only a wipe each week as part of your fridge clean.

You will need

lemon juice or vinegar in a spray bottle
1 tbsp table salt
1–2 tbsp bicarb
soft cloths
old toothbrush

Lemon juice and vinegar will kill mould and mildew. Spray along seals with vinegar or lemon juice and follow with a damp cloth dipped in salt to clean and kill the mould spots. After wiping down, if you have any remaining stubborn stains, attack with a dab of bicarb and then an abrasive rub with your forefinger inside the cloth, getting it in between the creases and folds of the door seal. You may need an old toothbrush to get into any difficult areas. A final wipe with warm soapy water and your fridge seals will be clean, whitened and free of unsightly black mould.

If you give the seals a weekly wipe down with lemon juice as part of your fridge maintenance, mould and mildew will not reappear and if you lapse at any point you can return to this recipe.

CLEANING COPPER PANS, CASSEROLES AND KETTLES

I have a beautiful set of copper pans that I have had for many years. I remember being desperate for these pans. It was fashionable to have them hanging from a rack. They were expensive, too, and I bought one pan per month until I had a full set. They are fantastic to work with but, due to the inevitable humidity in a kitchen, they quickly tarnish. The pans hanging from the rack looked so unsightly when not sparkling, so I took the rack down and now keep them in a cupboard. Cleaning these copper pans has always been way down on my list of cleaning priorities.

I used to buy a proprietary cleaner which, apart from not being environmentally friendly, was also very expensive. I would use it sparingly and rarely because of the cost rather than the harm to the environment.

When I started out on this journey, I became shocked once I understood how many harmful chemicals are included in so many things that are part of our everyday life. Many metal cleaners disclaim any harm to the environment unless they enter the waterways. Of course they will enter our waterways – many of the cleaners have to be washed off!

My copper pans were in need of some serious attention, my very expensive cleaner had run out and, when I looked at the eco-friendly proprietary choices, they too were expensive. I took to the internet and invested some serious time in researching, reading and watching YouTube videos from people promising quick, effective natural cleaning methods.

I have tried so many. From dipping a lemon in salt and rubbing that over, to bicarb with lemon juice, to rubbing tomato sauce over the pans and even a cola overnight soak. The one underlying theme is acid. Citric acid from lemon juice and acetic acid from the vinegar contained in tomato sauce are the agents that will dissolve the tarnish.

I discovered that an overnight soak in equal parts cola and vinegar does work, followed by a polish with a paste of bicarb and a soft cloth, but when there is a whole set of pans to clean, your bucket will only cope with one pan at a time and I needed pints and pints of cola and vinegar for my largest casserole. I felt I had to come up with something quicker if my pan cleaning was to take less than a week!

Inspiration for this recipe arose when I developed my toilet cleaner, of all things! After dissolving citric acid and water in a pan I noticed that the tiniest drip down the outside edge of the pan after pouring immediately dissolved the tarnish.

I had the starting point for my copper-cleaning recipe, but a watery solution on its own wasn't enough – it had to be thick enough to stick and spread around, and the addition of a little eco-friendly washing-up liquid did just that.

I know that not everyone will have a full set of copper pans, but because proprietary cleaners can be so expensive, are not kind to the environment and this tip is so helpful, I felt the urge to share. Of course, the recipe will also be quick and effective in cleaning the base of those pans fitted with just a copper bottom.

How often do I need to clean copper pans?

With this fantastic recipe I now clean my pans once a month.

You will need

100g citric acid
50ml water
15ml eco-friendly washing-up liquid/dish soap
glass bottle with spray attachment
small saucepan and wooden spoon
small funnel
rubber gloves
sponge
old toothbrush
fine wire wool

This recipe makes sufficient cleaner for a full set of pans (in my case, four pans with lids and a casserole dish with lid). Take the smallest saucepan and add the measured amount of citric acid and water. Stir with the wooden spoon over a low heat until the citric acid dissolves and you have a clear syrup. This doesn't take long – there is no need to boil the liquid. Use the funnel to transfer the warm syrup to a glass bottle, then add the washing-up liquid.

Apply the spray attachment to the bottle and start work.

I do the cleaning at the sink. Have a bowl of warm soapy water at the ready. Spray over the lids and, with gloved hands, spread the cleaner all over the surface so that the whole lid has a covering. Set aside for a minute or two. For pans, spray around the outside of the pan and again, use your hands to work the cleaner all over the surface. This enables the cleaner to get to work on the whole pan and not just where the spray marks are. After a couple of minutes, return to the original pan lid and use a sponge, old toothbrush and fine wire wool to work at any remaining tarnish. My pans were very badly stained, and one or two stubborn areas needed a further spot-spray.

Pop the lids and pans into the bowl of soapy water to rinse away the cleaner, dry with a soft cloth and see your reflection!

The recipe given is sufficient to clean a number of pans. If you have an amount of cleaner left in the bottle, there's no need to discard it. The cleaner will keep in the bottle, but before storing away, rinse the spray attachment and flush it through with clean water. Pop a screw top on the bottle and store the spray attachment separately. Any citric acid left in the spray mechanism will crystallize and the trigger to the spray will fix.

If you forget to flush out the spray, and the next time you come to use the cleaner it refuses to spray, simply unscrew the spray attachment, pop it into a jug and pour over recently boiled water from the kettle. Leave for a minute or so and the citric acid will dissolve and the spray will be working again.

RHUBARB LEAVES FOR
CLEANING POTS AND PANS

This is a great way to clean the inside of your pans and shine up tarnished lids.

Just as citric acid is naturally found in citrus fruits and acetic acid in vinegar, sour rhubarb contains oxalic acid, and it is more concentrated in the leaves. After trimming the stalks, use the leaves – about four leaves torn into pieces and boiled in a pan half-full of water for at least 10 minutes will clean your stained pans and pan lids. To clean a lid, submerge the lid into a pan larger than the lid itself.

I have a number of saucepans and lids that benefit from this treatment – the tarnish and stain just lift from the inside. Do not use this recipe on pans with a non-stick lining. The treatment did not rid my enamel casserole dish of stains – much to my disappointment.

If you have stained enamel or cast iron cook or bakeware it can be restored to its former glory, see next tip.

CAST IRON CASSEROLES AND ENAMEL BAKEWARE

I have a number of beautiful coloured cast iron casseroles. They are super handy in the kitchen because they can be transferred from the hob to the oven and then to the table – a fantastic piece of kit that will last a lifetime. However, the outside and the inside can look unsightly and not really suitable for serving from when really grubby. Similarly, I have the traditional white enamel pie plates and pudding dishes, the ones with a blue border. I think maybe most kitchens have one lurking somewhere but, again, they become stained even though they may be perfectly clean.

I have two methods – one for cleaning the shiny beautiful outside of cast iron (e.g. Le Creuset) type casseroles and pans and a second for the stained insides of these and enamelware.

How often do I need to de-stain casseroles and enamel?

As and when stains occur, otherwise no more than once a year.

You will need

TO CLEAN THE OUTSIDE
120g washing soda
hot water
2–3 tbsp bicarb
fine wire wool

TO CLEAN THE INSIDE
1–2 tbsp green bleach
boiling water

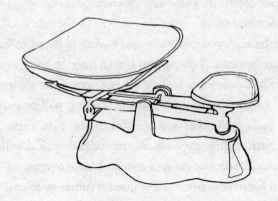

To clean the outside

Use a bowl or sink and sprinkle in the washing soda then pour over hot water. I find this is a quick and efficient method for dissolving the crystals. Adding the crystals to the hot water results in having to stir until they are dissolved. Fill the bowl to about 3 inches (7cm) deep then stand the casserole in it so that the water comes up the sides and covers any burnt-on deposits and marks. The weight of the casserole ensures it stands in the bowl without floating. Leave overnight.

Next day, pour away the water and use the fine wire wool dipped in bicarb to work at any remaining marks – they will have softened and will readily clean off.

To remove stains on the inside of enamelware, casseroles and pans

This can be achieved easily without having to resort to harmful chemicals. Sprinkle 2 tbsp green bleach into the base for a large casserole and pour over boiling water to cover the stained area. Leave 3 hours or overnight and the staining will be gone. For smaller pans, casseroles and pie dishes and plates use 1 tbsp green bleach and for even smaller items, ½ tbsp. Fill with boiling water to cover the stained area and leave overnight.

Green bleach doesn't smell or give off fumes so after the soak I tip away the solution down the sink and rinse my spotlessly clean casseroles, pans and enamelware in warm water then dry with a cloth.

HOME

There are so many cleaning jobs to do around the home, and I used to pride myself on my range of goodies. Furniture polish spray, floor cleaner, window cleaner, upholstery cleaner, stain removal, carpet stain removers, aerosol room-freshener spray, single-use impregnated perfumed wipes – the list went on and on.

Then I made the decision to go green and challenge myself to come up with alternatives for anything and everything that presented me with a cleaning problem. The result – I have saved money! I am amazed when I consider the amount of money I used to spend on cleaning products, each one with its own specialism, which I believed were doing a fantastic cleaning job around the house. Of course I knew that vinegar was good for windows and bicarb was a great 'all-rounder', but I genuinely believed that these simple products had been replaced by better, more up-to-date specific and efficient modern upgrades.

I now realize, through further reading and practice, how misinformed I was. Chemical cleaners and their packaging are unnecessary and expensive, and the vast majority I can think of are actually causing more harm than good.

WINDOW CLEANING

We all have our pet cleaning hates, and mine is cleaning the windows. Consequently, my windows are often very grubby before they get the necessary treatment.

Outside windows and inside windows tend to have different types of grime. On the outside there will be dust and debris that has blown onto them as well as dried rain marks, and on the inside there could be cobwebs, grease (especially on kitchen windows) and dried condensation marks.

Vinegar is fantastic for glass as it cleans, cuts through grease and will wipe out any water marks. Newspaper used to be great for polishing glass after the vinegar wipe, but fewer people buy a newspaper nowadays, so I have opted for a clean polishing cloth instead – both work well.

How often do I need to clean the windows?

I try to clean windows once a month but, if I am honest, every three months is more accurate as it is the one job I detest!

You will need

very soft bristled brush (from a dustpan and brush set)
bucket of warm water with a squirt of eco-friendly washing-up
   liquid/dish soap and a cloth
glass spray bottle of white vinegar
dry polishing cloth

Whether cleaning outside or inside windows, start with a good brush down. If you have never thought to do this before, remember there will be dust on windows, especially on the outside, along with cobwebs and other debris. Brushing away any dust while it is dry will make cleaning much easier. Dust and cobwebs can be very difficult to clean once wet.

Take a bucket of warm soapy water, wring out the cloth and work at wiping the window, starting at the top and working all the way down. Rinse the cloth once or twice depending on how dirty the window is (you will see from your cloth). Wipe glazing bars and paintwork at the same time.

Then take the vinegar, give a couple of sprays directly onto the glass and use the damp cloth again to wipe over. Using the soft polishing cloth, dry and shine up your glass. Outside windows will dry quickly, so polish with your dry cloth before the vinegar has had a chance to dry.

On the inside the opposite is true, and the windows will not dry quickly, so a thorough polish until dry is important for streak-free glass.

Window cleaning is my least favourite job of all, but trying to rush and cut corners can actually make the windows look worse than before I started. I have, in the past, been persuaded by a spray-on, wipe-off all-in-one cleaning product, which may be fine if the glass isn't too grubby, but this isn't the case when it comes to my windows and glass.

My way is to choose a dull day – don't try to clean windows when the sun is shining on them as they dry quickly before there has been any chance to polish them, resulting in streaks. I get the music on, then start! My favourite songs keep me going and my largest, dirtiest windows get the full treatment without me even realizing.

My windows are clean, everything is clear and bright and I vow to never let them get that bad again . . .

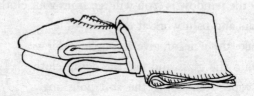

CLEANING SMALL AND LARGE BRASS ITEMS

I have a whole range of brass items in my home including door handles, stair rods, brass light fittings, window catches, a fender, kettle and dustpan and brush!

I used to reach for the chemical wadding and, although it carried huge environmental warnings, I never even considered that when I rinsed off the chemicals I was polluting our rivers and waterways as all the nasties were being poured down my sink.

I allow brass to tarnish quite badly because like so many cleaning jobs, it's not until it becomes a problem that we notice! Moisture in the atmosphere tarnishes brass in the same way that it affects copper and silver.

I did my research and concluded that different brass items around my home needed different cleaning methods.

How often do I need to clean the brass?

My brass items tend to get a clean twice a year.

You will need

FOR SMALL ITEMS (WINDOW CATCHES, SMALL DOORKNOBS)

100ml white vinegar

bicarb

small cup or bowl

fine wire wool

old toothbrush

soft cloth

FOR ITEMS TOO LARGE TO DROP INTO A SOLUTION (STAIR RODS, FENDERS)

3 tbsp bicarb

warm water

table salt

large old towel

sponge or fine wire wool

rubber gloves

FOR LARGE OR SMALL INTRICATE ITEMS (BRASS FIRE FURNITURE AND KETTLES)

100g citric acid

50ml water

10ml eco-friendly washing-up
   liquid/dish soap

table salt

small saucepan

wooden spoon

funnel

reusable glass bottle with
   spray attachment

rubber gloves

old toothbrush

sponge

soft cloth to dry and polish

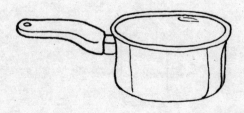

Small items

Any small, handy brass items can be cleaned quite quickly. I have window catches, for example, which are very small – small enough to sit in the bottom of a cup. Pour over white vinegar, enough to cover and leave for an hour or two. Mine were badly tarnished, as you might guess, so I left them overnight. The next day I used a piece of dampened wire wool dipped into a little bicarb and an old toothbrush for creases, rubbing lightly around a couple of stubborn areas. Rinsed in warm soapy water and dried with a soft cloth, these catches shined up a treat.

Large, awkward or immovable items

I have a brass fire fender and stair rods, all of which are large, awkward items. I tend to take a large dog towel, on with the rubber gloves, and lay it on a work surface or table, or in the case of immovable items – around the item itself. In a small bowl mix together the bicarb and warm water to a smooth, thin paste then dot onto the brass and leave for 5–10 minutes before rubbing away the tarnish with a sponge. Any difficult areas can be tackled by dipping the sponge or fine wire wool in table salt. This provides a slight abrasive to clean away any difficult bits. Clean off the paste in warm soapy water, then dry with a clean polishing cloth.

Large, intricate items

I have a fairly ornate, very old brass dustpan and brush which, because of its shape, I rarely get around to giving a thorough clean. Even when I used to use wadding and proprietary chemical cleaners, I found it difficult to get into every nook and cranny. My own recipe is actually the fastest-acting, cheapest and best cleaner I have ever used.

Take a small saucepan and add the citric acid and water and place over a gentle heat, stirring until the citric acid dissolves and you have a clear syrup. Use the funnel to transfer the liquid into a glass bottle, then add the eco-friendly washing-up liquid. Apply the spray attachment and get to work.

Spray all over the item, then use gloved hands to massage the liquid all around and into every nook, crease and cranny, using an old toothbrush to get into difficult areas. Leave for 2–3 minutes, then use a sponge to rub away at the tarnish. On any difficult areas dip the sponge in salt and use as a natural non-scratch scourer.

Once the tarnish has dissolved, simply rinse off the soapy cleaning solution then wash the article in warm soapy water (simply eco-friendly washing-up liquid) and rinse and dry with a soft cloth.

NOTE: Make up sufficient solution to do the work in one go. After use, rinse the bottle, and more importantly the spray attachment, in clean water. Otherwise the citric acid will crystallize in the nozzle and seize up. If you forget and the next time you return to the nozzle it has jammed, do not panic – for a tip on freeing a seized nozzle, see page 126.

SILVER CLEANING: JEWELLERY, SILVERWARE AND PHOTO FRAMES

My clean and green journey has been fun as I have discovered simple, easy and effective alternatives. I have had my disasters, too! Common practice in my house was to invest in branded silver dips, polishes and wadding. While being quite expensive, it was only when I examined the packaging and labels and delved further to read their Safety Data Sheets that I realized the ones I used were also flammable, toxic and considered harmful to the environment.

I don't have a vast amount of silver, just a few small items: three silver photo frames, silver cutlery and a pair of silver earrings (I'm a gold girl, myself!). By the way, don't be tempted to clean silver rings with stones in this way. The solution and chemical reactions could affect the stones. To clean silver rings with stones, I would prefer you follow the cleaning instructions for gold (see pages 244–5).

How often do I need to clean the silver?

When tarnish appears – I clean silver items about every three to four months.

You will need

bicarb
aluminium foil

kettle of boiling water
soft cloth

The easiest, quickest and most effective natural silver-cleaning method is as follows. No scratching, rubbing or abrasion. Have a look at the items you need to clean. I have the silver screw top from a vintage sugar shaker. The base is glass but the top is silver and very tarnished. My second item is a small christening mug and the third is the top and spoon from my grandmother's glass jam pot.

Next, find a bowl that will take the items comfortably so that they are not overlapping or resting on each other. Then take a roll of aluminium foil and line the bowl, making sure the dull side is touching the bowl and the shiny side will be touching the items to be cleaned. I find it easier to mould the foil around the outside of the bowl then transfer it to the inside – there is less risk of the foil tearing.

This is where it gets exciting. Place the items in the foil-lined bowl, add a tablespoon of bicarb and put the kettle on. Once the water has boiled, pour it immediately onto the items in the bowl making sure everything gets covered in the fizzing water. Leave for only a few minutes, and see the tarnish just lift off! Don't burn your hands as you lift the items from the bowl. Then just rinse, dry and polish everything with a soft duster. This is great for those items with lots of nooks and crannies and for cutlery and jewellery – well, anything really – except photo frames!

While I am not an enquiring scientist, I did wonder how this works. I noticed the foil turned grey and there were tiny deposits at the bottom of the bowl. On further reading I am given to understand that a reaction between silver sulphide and aluminium occurs when the two are immersed in a hot bicarb solution. The reaction transfers the sulphur from the silver and it adheres to the aluminium.

I had to check for myself that the foil was indeed the game changer, so I placed a tarnished silver cup in a bowl without foil and used only a tablespoon of bicarb, poured over boiling water and you've guessed it – nothing happened.

What to do about those items that cannot be submerged in water? My photo frames are the first things to look unsightly when tarnished, but the first time I worked my natural clean on them was somewhat disastrous.

I had read that bicarb mixed to a paste with lemon juice would remove silver tarnish. I mixed the paste, thrilled at the fizz and set to with a cloth on my silver picture frame. Nothing seemed to happen, so I took a pan-scouring pad, working it vigorously around my precious frame. You have probably guessed the outcome. The tarnish had disappeared but so had the shiny silver finish. My photo frame is now badly scratched!

My advice is as follows: do not believe everything you read on the internet, and do not mix lemon juice and bicarb together to clean silver. Lemon juice is acid and bicarb is alkaline, and when they come together they make that gorgeous fizz as they cancel each other out to make a neutral base. In the case of these two natural chemicals, they produce carbon dioxide gas, water and salt.

All you need to clean your silver picture frames is bicarb and a soft, damp cloth. I find it easier to lay an old towel on the worktop, giving a soft surface to work on. Simply put 2 tbsp bicarb in a saucer and with a couple of fingers in a dampened cloth, dip them into the bicarb then work on the photo frame in small circular motions. The tarnish will lift off onto the cloth, which will begin to stain black. Keep moving your fingers around in the cloth, dabbing on more bicarb as you work your way around the frame. Finally, when the frame is shiny and sparkling (and not scratched), simply buff it up with a clean, dry duster.

CLEANING SILVER: 'UPCYCLING'

This tip is borrowed from the previous tip, but is so handy and quick and avoids single-use aluminium foil; it's a fantastic quickie for cleaning up prongs on tarnished forks or any small silver items.

You will need

1 tsp bicarb
boiling water
1 washed aluminium can

I have a canteen of silver-plated cutlery which comes out at Christmas and on special occasions, and even though it looks shiny and good, the prongs of the forks tend to blacken.

I used to get out the silver wadding full of chemicals, but I now reach for yesterday's baked-bean tin. Choose a non-coated aluminium can, remove the label and give the tin a thorough wash. Pop the tarnished forks into the tin, prongs end down, add 1 tsp bicarb and pour over boiling water.

Take care: the liquid will fizz and rise briefly to the top of the can, so only half fill it with water. Leave for 1–2 minutes. Remove your forks, rinse under the tap, dry and pop onto your table, ready for dinner.

This is upcycling at its best!

WOOD FURNITURE: MY FURNITURE POLISH

For probably the whole of my adult life, or at least the part of my adult life that has involved cleaning (which is most of it), I have purchased aerosol cans of furniture polish. Easy, convenient, smells good and not too expensive. Once I'd embarked on my clean and green journey, I decided to do some reading around wood furniture polishing products.

Not until I read a newspaper article some time ago did I begin to question the use of aerosol sprays. My head was spinning when I read about their effect on solar radiation and cloud properties, and that aerosol particles affect air quality and, hence, have an effect on human health and well-being. A lot of the reading got too heavy for me, but the main message coming through was easy enough to understand and I decided to change my products immediately. I considered my use of aerosol polish and my busy cleaning routine during which I must have been happily inhaling the particulate ingredients week after week.

Further reading suggested that aerosol spray polish may not be doing my wood furniture any good either. Continuous use can actually lift a wood veneer over time, though I never knew this. I decided to make my own polish.

How often do I need to use wood polish?

Use weekly on wood furniture.

You will need

50ml groundnut, vegetable or sunflower oil, the thinnest
   variety you have (or even better, home-made lavender oil –
   see pages 176–8)
30ml white vinegar
30 drops organic lavender essential oil
funnel
300ml glass reusable bottle with spray attachment

Simply measure all the ingredients into a glass bottle with
a spray attachment. I have used olive oil and rapeseed oil in
the past, but have found the thinner groundnut, vegetable or
sunflower oils give a better result. The thinner the oil the finer
your furniture spray polish. Give the polish a good shake before
each use and it is good to go. I like the classic smell of lavender
in polish, but use drops of any organic essential oil to suit your
taste – orange works well.

A little goes a long way, and you will find a spray or two onto a soft cloth or duster then a polish over your wood furniture items will bring them up a treat. I have many old pieces of wood furniture and they looked rich, nourished and shiny after using my polish. The oil in the polish will feed and nurture the wood, the white vinegar will help kill any bacteria, clean with a shine and cut through any greasy marks, and the essential oils have antiseptic and perfume properties of their own. I adore that clean 'just polished' smell when you re-enter a room. I love it! This is also an excellent cleaning product for stainless steel.

If, like me, you become addicted to a clean and green lifestyle, then I urge you to make your own lavender oil and use it in this polish. It is fun to make – in fact, it makes itself – the oil turns a purple colour and smells gorgeous.

WALNUTS FOR WOOD SCRATCHES

Scratches happen on furniture and wood flooring and a quick and easy method to fill and cover them is to use a walnut. Take a whole walnut, break it in half and use the raw side to rub the scratch. Rub the nut across rather than in the same direction of the scratch and you will see the scratch fill and literally disappear. Any greasy mark left on the wood can be polished off with a soft cloth.

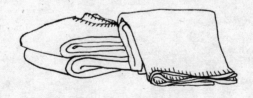

NANCY'S NATURAL NURTURE
(FOR LEATHER GOODS OF ANY COLOUR)

This treatment will restore and replenish any leather goods of any colour. I have used it on my leather sofa, leather cushions, red shoes and adorable twenty-year-old leather walking boots.

How often do I need to restore leather goods?

This could be a one-off treatment. My sofa suffers light damage from direct sunlight, so I treat it every year. Shoes, boots, handbags and jackets may need just the one treatment.

You will need

TO CLEAN
bowl of warm water
squirt of eco-friendly washing-up liquid/dish soap
2–3 tbsp vinegar
4 tbsp bicarb (for boots and shoes)
small brush or cloth

TO NURTURE
50g coconut oil to moisturize
food colour gel to match item (optional)
20ml vegetable glycerine to soften
20 drops organic essential oil (lemon or clove bud)
  – contains antifungal properties plus perfume

small bowl

spoon or tiny whisk to mix

soft, absorbent cloth

Use on leather furniture that has suffered light damage or has cracked and become dry due to central heating. Great for leather walking and hiking boots that have been neglected and have dried leaving mouldy patches. Wonderful for that old but favourite handbag or pair of shoes – in fact, any leather item into which you want to inject new life.

In the case of boots or shoes, make sure they are clean before starting. Boots or shoes that have mould or dirt should be washed first using a brush or cloth and warm soapy water with vinegar added. The vinegar, as well as helping to clean the leather, will help kill any mould spores.

If the shoes or boots have odour on the inside, once the outsides have been washed then pop 2 tbsp bicarb into each boot. Give it a shake around then leave the boots outside to air-dry and freshen up – windy dry sunny days are perfect.

Once dry, shake and knock out any bicarb, then the nurturing can begin.

Start with semi-soft coconut oil. Kept in a cool place, coconut oil is solid and white but at just above room temperature (28°C approximately) it softens like butter. This is the perfect consistency. Measure 50g into a small bowl then use a tiny whisk or teaspoon to mix in food colour gel. Don't go too dark at this stage – more colour can be added later after a patch colour test. If the colour of your leather item is good then there is no need to add colour to the cream.

Once well blended, mix in the vegetable glycerine and finally the essential oil. The cream is now ready to use. If a colour gel has been added to the cream, test a little on the item to check the match and then start work. Use a soft cloth to massage the cream into the leather.

If the leather is dry the cream will be absorbed quickly, but in any event leave the item for an hour or so to absorb. It may seem that the leather looks greasy and sticky but don't be alarmed, the leather will drink up the cream. A second coat can then be applied. Leave for around 2 hours before rubbing the leather with your hands. Any greasy feel will have disappeared, the leather will have absorbed the cream and be feeling soft, plush and wholesome.

I used this method for all of the following.

I have a dark brown leather sofa. It is many years old and from time to time when it looked tired I would treat it to a makeover! It suffers light damage because it belongs in my conservatory and sunlight causes it to crack and fade. In the past I have bought leather restoration kits, some retailing for as much as £30 a time and often containing not quite enough to treat a whole sofa. I decided to make my own treatment and am so pleased, so much so I have given it a name: Nancy's Natural Nurture. What started as an experiment has proved to be a beautiful, inexpensive, long-lasting treatment for leather at probably less than a quarter of the cost of a branded kit.

My sofa was badly scratched, marked and faded. As it is dark brown in colour, my first thoughts were to rub over shoe polish, but having done this once before to an old blue leather car seat I remembered that the polish does rub off on clothing. White jeans and blue shoe polish don't go well together! My sofa now gets an annual treatment using my brown cream, the colour doesn't rub off on clothing and the leather looks and feels as good as the day it was bought. I leave the sofa for 2–3 hours to allow the treatment to be absorbed, then replace the fabric seat cushions and it looks wholesome and happy.

Another time I considered discarding an old pair of leather boots. Nostalgia got the better of me and a few hours later they had taken on renewed elegance and are being worn again regularly. The frayed laces were trimmed and sealed over a naked flame and the boots, washed and cleaned of mould, then enjoyed three coats of the gorgeous cream.

I had a pair of red leather shoes, but then a spill or splash of something (no idea what) left me with a pair of shoes but in two different colours. A treatment with my red-coloured cream and I have a matching pair again.

SPILLS, MARKS AND STAINS ON WHITE FURNITURE, INCLUDING NAIL VARNISH

White furniture, whether it be melamine, shiny, glossy composite material or painted wood, will show spills, marks and stains quickly. Nail varnish smudges or spills of nail varnish can create a panic. Removing colour residue from old Post-its or wax crayon on children's bedroom furniture can at first sight seem an impossible task.

I have over the years had bedroom furniture in children's bedrooms that has suffered all types of abuse, from wax crayons when they were small to nail varnish and model transfers as they got older. I now have a white table in a spare bedroom used for craft projects, and that suffers spills, too.

How often do I need to remove stains from white furniture?

This works on old and new stains.

You will need

toothpaste (many products are eco-friendly)
soft, slightly damp micro cloth

Toothpaste comes to the rescue. Simply massage it over the stain, leave for 15 minutes then clean off. Non-scratch, no rubbing and making dull – the stains wipe off easily. Having done some reading around using toothpaste as a stain remover, it is evident that many products contain my green and clean staples – bicarb and surgical spirit.

One follower messaged me in a panic when a bottle of fake tan had leaked over her white furniture. I suggested toothpaste and it worked.

SPOT-CLEAN STAINS ON CARPETS

I have named this tip simply 'spot stains' because there are those occasions when, during the course of your cleaning, you come across a carpet stain. No idea what it is or how long it has been there. If in any doubt though, try my 'go-to' option on p. 158 first as it's more gentle.

How often do I need to spot-clean the carpet?

This is a one-off, but surprisingly lifts many carpet stains.

You will need

bicarb
warm water
small bowl
cloth

In my spare bedroom I have a pale cream carpet. The room is rarely used, but then I came across two stains – absolutely no idea what they were, so I was unsure how to treat them. They were dark spot stains – could be tea or coffee, could be make-up. I decided to give them a dab with a soft cloth and warm water but nothing shifted, so instead I reached for the bicarb and mixed 2 tbsp with warm water to a thin paste, dabbed that onto each stain, massaged it in gently and just left it to dry. The next day I vacuumed the dry powder, rubbed the place over with a lightly dampened clean cloth and the stains disappeared.

This method also works on old, dried-in wine stains and vomit, urine and other spoils from children and pets. I discovered a red wine stain under a chair also on a cream carpet, and the same mix and method was applied.

Anyone who has children or pets will I am sure be faced with a clean-up job at some time. Children and pets have accidents and many items can be cleaned up, soaked in cold water then popped into the washing machine. This can include bedding, towels and clothing, but what about when the stain or smell is lingering on a carpet or mattress? Don't be tempted to reach for strongly perfumed disinfectants, because the odour plus the perfume when they come together can make the smell even worse. The odour needs to be neutralized, and believe it or not the most effective remedy is bicarb.

Mix a thin paste and dab it over the stain, massaging it in circular motions with gloved hands. The residual stain will lift and so will the odour. If you can air-dry the item, even better.

NOTE: When dealing with carpet stains, never be tempted to give the carpet a vigorous rub and scrub because this can damage the pile. I speak from experience here, as I once dived straight onto a stain with a cloth and a full jar of elbow grease. I rubbed and scrubbed at this stain, only to find when everything had dried that the stain had disappeared but was replaced by a permanently damaged scuffed carpet pile. Remember: however bad the stain, gently does it.

TEA, COFFEE AND OTHER SPILLS ON CARPETS AND UPHOLSTERY

As with most spills, quick action is best. Tea or coffee left to dry completely will be more difficult to remove, and dried-in drinks containing milk can leave a sour odour. I have found this solution to be excellent for so many stains. Pet stains, wine, fruit juice and more – it's my go-to for most spills.

How often do I need to clean tea and coffee spills?

As quickly as possible after the spill.

You will need

2 tbsp white vinegar
1 tbsp eco-friendly washing-up liquid/dish soap
tepid water
absorbent paper
small bowl
cleaning cloth

Quickly mop up as much of the tea or coffee as possible using absorbent paper. Do not rub or scrub but carefully push the paper into the spill and soak it up. When the spill is on a carpet, I stand on the paper until there is no further wetting.

In a small mixing bowl place the vinegar and washing-up liquid, then add sufficient tepid water to fill the bowl about half-full. Add your cloth to the bowl and head over to the remaining stain.

Using the cleaning cloth wrung out of the vinegar solution, start at the outside of the stain and work inward, dabbing and gently massaging. Rinse the cloth and wring it out regularly and continue patiently until the stain has disappeared. The washing-up liquid will clean the stain and the vinegar will ensure there is no residual odour. Leave the stain to dry completely. Whether working on a carpet stain or upholstery, do not be tempted to vigorously rub at the pile or fabric. You may find you have cleaned the stain but permanently damaged your furniture or carpet. Gently does it.

CANDLE WAX SPILL ON CARPET
OR SOFT FURNISHINGS

Candle wax spills happen, and although I tend to only use candles at Christmastime I have had many occasions when spills have appeared on tablecloths and hard surfaces, but worst of all on my plain cream carpet.

You will need

bicarb
brown paper or brown envelopes larger than the plate of
   your iron
an iron
damp cloth

Melted wax should be left to harden before attempting to do anything with it, otherwise the problem will be worsened if you spread the wax by trying to mop it up. Even though I watched the candle wax soak into my plain cream carpet, I refrained from rubbing it or trying to mop it up.

Once completely hard to the touch, reach for the brown paper. Any brown paper will do – I have even ripped up used brown envelopes for the job. You may need quite a lot, depending on the size of the spill. Brown paper usually has a shiny side and a dull side – lay the dull side onto the spill, plug in and switch on your iron.

Once the iron has come to a wool temperature, carefully iron over the paper and you will see the wax begin to stain the paper as the heat from the iron melts it. Move the paper around, ironing over the stain as you go. Take care though – make sure your iron doesn't come into direct contact with the carpet or the wax, as you will have created a clean-up problem on your iron plate. In time the stain on the brown paper will get less and less until you have absorbed every last drop. Examine your carpet to make sure there are no residual stains, then turn the power off the iron and unplug it.

If the plate of your iron has browned, simply wait for your iron to cool, dip a damp cloth in a teaspoon of bicarb and rub onto the plate of your cold iron and the brown stain will just wipe off.

CAUTION: If your carpet is nylon make sure you have plenty of brown paper laid over it, otherwise you could melt the fibres and make an even worse mess.

If a wax spill has appeared on a tablecloth or soft furnishings, like a cushion cover or removable furniture cover, then I lay an old towel or more brown paper under the fabric and place brown paper over the top of the spill, then treat as for carpets. The spill can then be absorbed quickly from both sides of the fabric.

A wax spill on upholstered furniture should again be allowed to go completely cold and firm up. Scrape away any excess with a knife then use absorbent brown paper and an iron, as before. Any residual greasy-looking stain can be removed with a re-usable cotton pad dipped in surgical spirit.

If a spill occurs on hard surfaces, again, wait for it to firm up then gently scrape up with a knife.

I have splashed candle wax onto a wall when blowing out a candle at the end of the day, blowing the melted wax at the same time as the flame! I used kitchen paper and a hairdryer to remove it once it had set. I held the piece of kitchen paper over the splashes then used my hairdryer to blow onto the paper. Once warm, the wax will melt and the paper will absorb the wax.

Never pour melted wax down the sink – it will immediately set and block your drains.

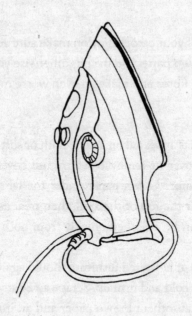

FRESHEN AND DRY-CLEAN YOUR CARPET

I have used this genius mix many times on my carpets. Bicarb neutralizes odours in your carpets from pets or just everyday living. By no means essential, but a great little addition is dried lavender (in the spring) or clove buds or cinnamon (great at Christmastime). These natural dried fragrances give a subtle, gentle fragrance to your room and your carpet.

I have a particular example. After winter, I give my lounge a thorough spring clean and move the winter log basket into the garage. It will stay there until it is required again at the end of the year. My carpet is pale cream, and the carpet under the log basket was cream and clean but the area around the basket was grubby from log debris when refuelling the fire. This called for a quick, eco-friendly dry shampoo.

How often do I need to freshen my carpet?

This can be either a once-a-year spring clean or whenever you think your carpet needs a refresh.

You will need

200g bicarb
2–3 tsp dried lavender, clove buds or a cinnamon stick broken
    into pieces
vacuum cleaner

glass sugar shaker (mine is a glass jar with a
    screw top with holes)
damp cloth

Place the bicarb in the jar and add the lavender,
clove buds or cinnamon, give it a shake and wait
for 24 hours for the natural scent to infuse, and it
is ready to use.

For a dry shampoo

Vacuum the carpet first, then apply a liberal sprinkle of the
lavender-scented bicarb mix followed by a gentle massage
into the pile using just the fingers. Leave the powder there
for 15–20 minutes, then take a damp cloth and gently work at
any carpet stains in small circular movements – do not rub the
carpet because the pile can be permanently damaged. Leave
overnight, then vacuum the next day. The carpet will be clean
and fresh.

For a general refresh

For example, to freshen up the carpet and get
rid of musty, tobacco or pet odours, sprinkle the scented bicarb onto the carpet then
gently rub into the carpet and leave for half
an hour. I sometimes leave mine overnight.
Vacuum the powder and the carpet and
room will smell fresh.

CARPET INDENTATIONS CAUSED BY FURNITURE

You have moved the room around or have decorated a room and want a change in layout. The problem is the carpet has dents in it where the furniture used to be. As much as you vacuum, the dints in the carpet remain. Or you may have moved house and taken on the previous owners' fitted carpets. Their furniture layout doesn't suit yours.

How often do I need to remove indentations in the carpet?

If ever you move a piece of furniture and there is an indent left where the chair or a table leg has been.

You will need

    clean tea towel
    steam iron
    fork (wooden is preferable)

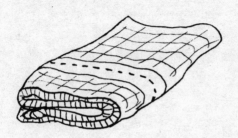

Using a clean cotton cloth or tea towel, lay it over the dent, then with your iron switched to the steam setting, iron over the dent, giving an extra puff of steam if your iron has that setting. Remove the tea towel. The steam will have loosened the pile. Then, using the fork the pile can be gently teased and lifted. Leave to dry and your carpet will be flawless.

If the carpets are nylon and you are not certain whether a hot iron is safe to use, then an ice cube left to melt on the squashed pile will lift the pile. If you have large areas of squashed-down pile, then the tea towel and iron is quicker and easier and won't soak your carpet.

CLEAN MARKS, FINGERPRINTS AND SMEARS ON SCREENS

We all make good use of our electronic devices – touchscreens in particular, whether that be our phone, tablet or satnav in the car. The TV screen, even though it doesn't suffer greasy fingerprints, does attract dust particles in the air due to the static electricity present. How many times have you wiped a layer of dust from your switched-off TV screen and wondered where that could have come from?

Rather than buying aerosol screen cleaners, single-use wipes or special mists, make up a bottle of your own.

How often do I need to clean the screens on my devices?

Clean once a week or as required.

You will need

150ml water
60ml white vinegar
40ml surgical spirit
few drops organic essential oil for perfume (optional – I used eucalyptus)
small plastic funnel
small glass bottle with fine spray nozzle
soft polishing cloth or clean duster

Made quickly and simply: pop the funnel into the neck of a small spray bottle, then add the measured ingredients. A light shake and it is good to go.

A fine spray on the screen – avoid spraying directly onto any speakers and vents – then buffing in a circular motion with a soft micro cloth will clear your computer, phone or car satnav screen in seconds. The vinegar will cut through any grease left from fingermarks, and along with the spirit will ensure any loitering bacteria are destroyed. The cleaner evaporates quickly, so no wet droplets. A further spray directly onto a cloth then a rub over the keyboard will clean away any dust and further debris and grease.

Vinegar eliminates static electricity, and a light, fine spray of the cleaner onto your TV screen will clean, remove the dust and help to prevent further dust particles collecting.

SPARKLY-CLEAN VASES AND DECANTERS

Whether it is a ship's decanter (narrow at the top and wide at the bottom) stained with residual dried red wine, a narrow-necked glass vase stained and cloudy at the base from old cut flower water or simply a reusable glass bottle with impossible deposits – these items can stain right at the base. My go-to fix was always a chlorine bleach solution! An overnight soak and the staining, in my mind, had disappeared. I realize now that the stain had been bleached but probably hadn't disappeared at all.

How often do I need to clean stained vases and decanters?

I should recommend every time your glass vase or decanter is used, though realistically I tend to use this tip as a treatment rather than a precaution.

You will need

- 2 tbsp bicarb
- 6 tbsp warm water
- 2 tbsp uncooked rice

I have used a number of eco-friendly methods to clean the bases of awkward glass items, all of which work. A tablespoon of builder's sand and a cup of water swirled around then tipped onto the garden; broken eggshells and a tablespoon of bicarb with water swirled around then tipped outside (not down the sink) also works.

The method I consider most accessible for most people is simply 2 tbsp bicarb, 6 tbsp warm water and 2 tbsp uncooked rice in the base of the decanter, vase or bottle. Give it a good shake and swirl around and then leave for 15 minutes. Discard the treatment down the sink (but be sure to catch and dispose of the rice), then flush with warm water and all is sparkling clean.

The process creates a natural scourer in the base of the vessel which cleans and polishes.

Keeping cut flowers in a vase after they have died results in the water discolouring and eventually turning sour and foul-smelling. Even after discarding the flowers on the compost heap the vase may be discoloured, slimy and very odorous. A tablespoon of bicarb sprinkled into the base of the vase then topped up with hot water and left overnight will clean the base and neutralize the odour.

SHINE UP DULL GLASSWARE

Cloudy glassware can look unsightly and fairly annoying if, for example, one of your set of six glass items is cloudy while the rest are shiny. The problem is usually one of two things. Either the cloudy film is the result of limescale, which could have been caused by the dishwasher. Or the discoloration is in fact tiny scratches, which can either be caused by the dishwasher, or it is actually a flaw and a sign that the glass is degrading – this can happen particularly with very old glass. This is a glass disease and is referred to as 'sick glass', which is an irreversible problem but one that can be covered up.

How often do I need to shine up the glassware?

Whenever you have cloudy, scratched or dull glassware.

You will need

   white vinegar
   coconut oil
   clean, soft polishing cloth

The first thing to do is to check whether the cloudy film is caused by limescale. Either submerge the glass in white vinegar or spray it inside and out with the vinegar and leave for 30 minutes. Rinse, dry and polish and any limescale should have dissolved.

If the cloudy film is still present, then the glass isn't cloudy due to limescale but because it has tiny scratches and imperfections. It can, however, be returned to its former glory quickly and simply.

Take the slightest smear of coconut oil onto a clean, soft cloth and wipe over the glass. The cloudy film is usually on the outside of the glass. Then use the same cloth to polish all over. The glass will be sparkling, twinkling and clear.

Unfortunately the fix isn't permanent, because after washing the cloudiness will return and your secret treatment will have to be repeated. It is a great fix to restore your perfect set of six glasses, and no one will ever know. There is no greasy film – the oil simply fills in the tiny cracks.

ALL-PURPOSE FLOOR CLEANER

My floors are tiled and, for that reason, I don't expect visitors to remove their shoes when they come round. Also, I have dogs and they have no idea whether their feet are dry, wet, muddy or otherwise. Consequently my floors on occasion do need a thorough clean.

I used to buy the strongest, most concentrated heavy-duty and heavily chemical cleaning fluids which promised to cut through grease and grime and leave my floors clean and germ-free.

By the time I wrote this recipe I was well down my clean and green road, and I remember considering what I needed from a floor-cleaning solution. It needed to do the job, I wanted foaming suds and I wanted a clean, fresh smell – and importantly, I didn't want it to cost any more than I was paying already.

How often do I need to clean a tiled floor?

I routinely mop the floor once a week, yet during the winter months, when the weather outside is wet and dirty, I sometimes find myself running around with the mop and bucket daily when muddy feet from humans and dogs have left their mark.

You will need

200ml white vinegar
50ml eco-friendly washing-up liquid/dish soap

30 drops organic essential oil (I have used clove bud, lemon,
    orange and eucalyptus)
funnel
300ml glass bottle with a screw top

This recipe is fantastic, it is easy to make at minimal cost (certainly less than anything on the market) and my 250ml mix is enough for about eight washes.

Simply funnel the above ingredients into the bottle and you're good to go. It is suitable for use on all floor types. (See note on wood floors, below.) White vinegar will help to kill germs and cuts through grease and grime. Eco-friendly washing-up liquid will provide happy bubbles and suds and will clean and shine wood floors, and essential oils, as well as providing perfume, also have their own antiseptic and cleaning properties.

The floor should be cleaned of dust and debris, then just 2 tbsp (30ml) of the concentrated cleaner added to a bucket. Half fill the bucket with hot water and you're ready to go. Mop the floors – dirt and marks will lift easily. Leave to dry naturally and pour the dirty water down the drain knowing no harm is being done to the environment.

NOTE: This floor cleaner is perfect for wood floors, though should be used slightly differently. After cleaning the floor of any dust and debris, simply place 30ml of the floor cleaner into a spray bottle with 100ml warm water. Spray the wood floor then mop with a dry or very slightly damp mop – no need to rinse off. The floor will dry without smears and without being slippery, and using a spray mist ensures the wood doesn't get too wet.

LEMON OR LAVENDER INFUSED OIL

I refer to organic essential oils many times in this book, and I considered trying to make my own until I read and realized that lots of specialist equipment is probably required, plus a good understanding of distilling and the science involved. I will continue to buy them!

Infused oils are easy to make, and will come in handy if you decide to make my furniture polish (see pages 146–8). If you are planning to use your infused oil in my furniture polish then the thinner the oil you use, the better. Olive oil can be very rich and thick whereas groundnut is thinner and more free flowing which makes for a fine spray, perfect for polish. Lemon oil is also delicious included in salad dressings and drizzled over pizza, and adds a subtle flavour to home-made pesto. Infused oil for eating will keep for up to three months in the fridge.

How often do I need to make infused oils?

Once a year.

You will need

LEMON OIL
240ml grapeseed oil (or olive or rapeseed oil)
5–6 lemons
small bowl
small saucepan

lemon zester or potato peeler
500ml glass jar with screw top

LAVENDER OIL
50g dried lavender
240ml groundnut or grapeseed oil (or olive or rapeseed oil)
coffee grinder or pestle and mortar
500ml glass jar with screw top

For the lemon oil
Place the measured amount of oil in a small bowl and sit it over
a pan of barely simmering water. Add the zests from five or six
lemons to the oil. I used a potato peeler for the zesting rather
than a fine grater. Stir well, submerging the zests, then put a
plate or lid over the bowl and leave the pan on the lowest
simmer – you don't want the oil to boil. Leave it ticking over
for 2 hours. After the simmering time, transfer the peels and
oil into a warm jar, screw the lid on and leave it on a light windowsill for two weeks, giving it a shake every day. After the two
weeks, strain the oil into clean jars and store in the fridge.

> **NOTE:** Do not add garlic, chilli or fresh herbs to home-made infused oil. This is a specialized area, and while adding citrus is safe for home infusing, adding other plant matter without following correct procedure can cause botulism.

For the lavender oil

Crush the lavender to extract as much of the perfume as possible. Use either a coffee grinder or a pestle and mortar – both do a great job. Pop the crushed lavender into a bowl and add the oil. Heat over a pan of barely simmering water, not allowing the oil to boil – just ticking over for 2 hours. Transfer the mixture into a jar with a screw top and leave for two weeks. After this time, strain the now dark, pungent oil into small jars and use a measured amount to make my furniture polish where the recipe calls for oil.

Infused lavender and lemon oils to be used in cleaning recipes will keep for a year in a cool, dark place.

FRESHEN THE AIR WHILE YOU CLEAN

I am not a fan of aerosol sprays, candles or gadgets that emit sweet-smelling chemicals into the room, but when I have cleaned a room I like to enjoy a clean smell. Having dogs, too, I think it is important to keep rooms well ventilated. Have you ever walked into a house where the smell that hits you first is a doggy smell?

How often do I need to freshen the air?

A handy tip to help your regular cleaning become a fresh-smelling experience.

You will need

few drops organic essential oil – I prefer lavender for this
cleaned vacuum filter

My vacuum cleaner recommends a regular wash of the removable filter, which I then dry thoroughly and replace. Just a few drops (don't overdo it) of your favourite essential oil added to the dry filter will give you an instant perfume lift, freshening the air in your room next time you clean.

For those vacuum cleaners that use a disposable filter, you can add a few drops of your favourite essential oil each time you replace it.

WATER MARKS ON FABRICS

Water marks will wash out of soft furnishings, provided they are washable fabrics, of course. In my case we had had a roof leak and the water had dripped through the ceiling and onto my new pale cream lampshade, leaving a brown water stain. The lampshade was not an expensive one and my initial thoughts were to throw it away and replace. Two things stopped me – first, it is one of a matching pair, so I would have had to buy two and secondly, I reminded myself that in my grandmother's day throwing away would not have been an option – the stain would have been removed. So I set to work, and I'm so pleased I did.

How often do I need to remove water marks?

A water mark on fabric, in my case a lampshade, can be easily remedied but I would wait for a dry day.

You will need

    2 tbsp white vinegar
    spray bottle of water
    small reusable cotton pad (make-up
       remover pad)

The water mark could have been removed easily if I had submerged the whole lampshade in a large bucket of water with a cup of white vinegar added. I couldn't do this because the lampshade was too large for any bucket and the fabric had been glued to the frame, so I feared the worst.

Instead, I chose a fine day so that I could treat the lampshade outside. I started by spraying the area around the stain with a fine water mist then worked at the water mark, which was significant, I might add, being about 8 inches (20cm) wide and the length of the whole shade – around 12 inches (30cm).

Taking a reusable cotton make-up remover pad soaked in white vinegar, I then dabbed and gently rubbed away at the brown stain, particularly the dark, distinct edge of the water mark. After some minutes the vinegar removed the stain.

Importantly, when working with any water mark, the whole item has to be dampened so that a second water mark doesn't form as the item dries. It was necessary for me to then lightly spray the whole lampshade with water once more, after treating the stain, as the initial spray with water had now dried out in places. I left it to air-dry and it was as good as new.

NOTE: Water marks can be removed from leather, too, using this method.

DEODORIZING ROOM AND FABRIC SPRAY

I have never been a fan of candles, room fresheners or aerosols that make the room smell fragrant. Partly because I have pets and partly because if anyone has breathing problems or is sensitive in any way, then synthetic fragrances are the last thing they need to be breathing in.

I dislike strong perfumes on my skin, too, so light body sprays are all that I use, never the strong, pungent fragrances.

I wrote this recipe out of necessity. I have a small study and two walls of it are completely filled with books. I love books, some old, some new, paperbacks and hardbacks. Trouble is, I have been using my study more often recently and have noticed that there is a fusty smell. I live in an old house, yet none of the other rooms has this odour, so I am putting it down to the fact that the old books whiff a bit.

In the summer months I regularly have windows open – after all, fresh air is the best room freshener – but what do I do when the weather does not permit a good freshen-up of the room? This deodorizing room spray is just perfect. It is natural, it dispels odours, is fresh and clean-smelling and does not use any harmful chemicals or synthetic fragrances. It is safe for humans and pets. Great for spraying onto doggy beds, and so on.

How often do I need to use a deodorizing room spray?

As necessary.

You will need

- 20 drops organic essential oil – I use lemon (clove bud oil is great for cooking smells)
- 150ml boiled and cooled water
- 25ml lemon juice
- reusable glass bottle with spray attachment
- funnel

Take a reusable glass bottle with fine spray attachment. I say fine because you want the spray to linger in the air for a little while rather than fall like rain droplets onto the floor.

Use the funnel to pop the essential oil drops into the bottle for fragrance, then add the water followed by the lemon juice. If using freshly squeezed lemon juice, pass it through a strainer first to remove any pulpy bits. A light shake of the bottle, then spray the freshener into the air in the room.

I gave my fusty-smelling room a good spray into the air above my head. I then left the room and returned a couple of hours later. The room smelt only very slightly fragrant but more importantly, the odour had disappeared.

As an aside, I tried a number of natural room freshener recipes – there are many to choose from. In the end this is why I decided to make my own. I must just share with you this experiment. I read online that a fantastic room freshener can be made from bicarb, warm water and lemon essential oil. Sounded great, so I mixed up a bottle and sprayed it around the room. The site explained that bicarb will neutralize any odours.

The fragrance was lovely. I left the room then re-entered a few hours later to see whether there had been a lasting effect. There had – there were white dried drips on all of my furniture! Not harmful, as the dried bicarb just wiped off, but even so the room was a mess. If you see a room freshener containing bicarb, my advice is to give it a miss!

DRY(ISH)-CLEANING OF FURNITURE AND SOFT FURNISHINGS

Specialist dry-cleaning of furniture and furnishings often involves aerosol sprays, solvents and chemicals which are toxic and mobile in the environment, and the chemical pollution they create may persist for decades due to their resistance to degradation. There is of course a cost, which can be significant if it involves a professional coming along to your home to do the job, so I decided to have a go myself.

How often do I need to dry-clean furniture and soft furnishings?

As required – as part of a spring clean or after decorating a room.

You will need

2 tbsp washing soda
2 tbsp eco-friendly washing-up liquid/dish soap
300ml warm water
bicarb in a sugar shaker (optional)
medium-sized mixing bowl
shower puff
dry towel

Start by measuring the washing soda and washing-up liquid into the bowl, then add the warm water. Swirl around with the hand until the crystals have dissolved. Add the shower puff and work at the solution until the suds rise to the surface and the bowl is filled with white suds.

Rub only the suds onto the upholstery and massage over the whole area with the shower puff. If the furniture being cleaned is pale-coloured, then a sprinkle of bicarb (about 1 tbsp in total over a square metre) can be added and massaged in further. A sprinkle of bicarb is also useful to work on stains and marks. Leave the furniture for 15 minutes, then return and rub over again with the shower puff. Use the dry towel to rub away the suds and any bicarb paste. The furnishings will be only very slightly damp and should be left to dry for a few hours before using. I used this method to clean my cream dining room chairs and have followers who have been delighted with results on upholstery in their homes, caravans and cars.

MISCELLANEOUS SCUFFS AND MARKS

When I say scuffs and marks on painted walls, you will know exactly what I mean when I explain. So many of our homes have plain walls, painted with emulsion paint. The look is clean, crisp and light. The walls can suffer scuff marks for a whole range of reasons. I remember carrying a suitcase up the stairs one time and a rubber wheel left a mark on the white wall. Similarly, shoes and trainers can leave a scuff mark on skirting boards and walls. Even the vacuum cleaner can leave a scuff mark on paintwork if the soft rubber edge is allowed to move along the white paintwork or wall.

I recall reaching for a branded spray chemical cleaner to attempt to remove a scuff mark on my pale pink emulsion-painted wall, only to find after spraying the mark then rubbing with a cloth that I had successfully removed not just the mark but also the paint and its colour. Bicarb is much more discerning – it removes only what you want it to.

How often do I need to remove scuff marks?

Such a quick fix – do it as required.

You will need

1 tbsp bicarb
damp cloth
small bowl

Have a walk around your house – I do this from time to time seeking out scuffs, smudges and marks on walls, skirting boards, in the fridge, on white goods, on white shoes and trainers and even on the car!

The best and most effective way to remove scuff marks is to simply use a damp cloth, and then with the index finger dip into a little dry bicarb in a bowl and use this to gently rub onto the scuff mark. Hardly any pressure is required – the unsightly mark will just lift.

Similarly, skirting boards and kick boards around the base of kitchen units suffer scuffs and marks – again, easily removed with a damp cloth and bicarb. That grease ring left on the kitchen shelf by the base of your olive oil bottle will refuse to move using a cloth on its own, but dab it into bicarb and the stubborn oil ring will disappear.

White trainers, tennis shoes and sports shoes manage to collect black scuffs from hard surfaces and gym equipment. A rub with a damp cloth dipped in bicarb will bring them back to fitness.

I have to confess, I had a collision with a rubber parking bollard, but before the person with whom I live was able to assess the damage I had rubbed off the offending rubber graze with good old bicarb and a damp cloth. I am sure many a marriage will be saved by this genius ingredient.

BATHROOM

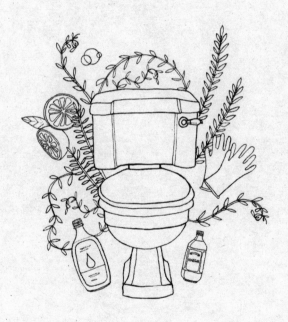

We all have a bathroom, shower room or toilet – whether it be the tiniest of spaces or a huge luxurious walk-in area. The cleaning issues are all the same whatever the room size. We need eco-friendly cleaners (such as my all-purpose cleaner, see pages 108–9) that will kill germs, dissolve limescale, kill mould, shift soap scum, shine up mirrors and glass, and smell clean too!

NANCY'S TOILET MAGIC

The development of this recipe wasn't straightforward because I found that the citric acid could crystallize in the base of the bottle after a couple of weeks. It can be dissolved again by heating, but I then discovered that adding the eco-friendly washing-up liquid not only added some froth to the cleaning solution (which always seems good!), it also emulsified the liquid and prevented the crystals re-forming. I also read that once citric acid crystals have been dissolved in water it is better to leave the bottle without a cap on for a few hours before sealing. I have been doing this and it seems to work, so I'll stick with it.

How often do I need to use Nancy's Toilet Magic?

The loo receives lots of attention from its users, and as a result needs to be given regular attention in return in order to keep it clean, fresh and germ-free. My loo gets a quick once-over every day and a thorough clean once a week (see pages 196–201).

You will need

200g citric acid
150ml just-boiled water
20ml eco-friendly washing-up
   liquid/dish soap
10–20 drops tea tree oil

1 pint measuring jug
small whisk
400ml glass bottle with
   spray attachment and
   screw top

Place the measured crystals in a heatproof measuring jug and pour over just-boiled water. Stir until the liquid is clear and the crystals have dissolved, then simply add the eco-friendly washing-up liquid and tea tree oil and mix well using a small whisk. Leave the liquid in the jug to cool completely and uncovered for a few hours then pour into a spray bottle and it is ready to use.

HOW TO CLEAN, FRESHEN, KILL GERMS AND DISSOLVE LIMESCALE IN THE LOO *WITHOUT* BLEACH

How to come up with an effective toilet-cleaning method that does the job, is economical and a natural alternative to bleach was probably my most frequently asked question. I tried many things and they all worked, but were either cumbersome or took too long. I remember standing for 20 minutes holding a cloth drenched in malt vinegar trying to dissolve the limescale at the back of the toilet bowl while not allowing the cloth to fall into the water. I recall boiling a kettle of water to pour into the toilet to give me hot water so that I could achieve a good clean.

The reader will be pleased to know that none of the above is necessary as I have streamlined the process. My main ingredient is citric acid, which is a fantastic natural cleaning product. It kills bacteria, mould and mildew, dissolves limescale, water stains, calcium deposits and rust. I added tea tree oil too – not only does it smell clean, but it has also been shown to kill certain bacteria, viruses and fungi.

I have decided to break the cleaning of the loo down into three parts – a quick daily, a thorough once-a-week clean and a one-off or troubleshooter loo clean.

You will need

FOR A DAILY SPRAY
spray bottle of Nancy's Toilet Magic (see pages 194–5)
toilet brush

FOR A FULL CLEAN
1–2 tbsp washing soda
bucket of hot soapy water (1 tbsp washing soda in hot water with
    a squirt of eco-friendly washing-up liquid/dish soap)
spray bottle of Nancy's Toilet Magic
rubber gloves
toilet brush
blue cloth reserved for cleaning the toilet
spray bottle of all-purpose cleaner (see pages 108-9)

FOR A ONE-OFF TREATMENT
1–2 tbsp washing soda
bucket of hot soapy water (1 tbsp washing soda dissolved in hot
    water with a squirt of eco-friendly washing-up liquid/dish soap)
2–3 tbsp citric acid crystals in a small bowl
spray bottle of Nancy's Toilet Magic
rubber gloves
toilet brush
blue cloth reserved for cleaning the toilet
old scourer

Daily spray

I find a routine of last thing at night or first thing in the morning works the best. Flush the toilet, then work around the bowl
and rim with a toilet brush. Spray Nancy's Toilet Magic inside

the bowl, paying particular attention to the back, where lime-scale deposits can begin to form. It is possible to sometimes see rivers where the water always runs and consequently where you will get a build-up of limescale. Give it a good brush again then leave the cleaning fluid on the bowl without flushing. The cleaner left without flushing will give time for the citric acid and tea tree oil to do their work.

NOTE: If you spray your toilet seat with toilet magic be sure to wipe it clean with a cloth. The citric acid can dry feeling sticky. I tend to use toilet magic for the bowl itself and use all-purpose cleaner for the seat, handle and outside of the toilet.

Full clean

This should be done once a week. On with the rubber gloves. I colour-code my cleaning cloths for the bathroom – pink for the sink and blue for the loo!

1 Start by flushing the toilet. Sprinkle the washing soda around the bowl. (The soda will adhere if the toilet has just been flushed.) Take the toilet brush and work the soda around the rim of the bowl and into the water, scrubbing vigorously. Flush the toilet again. This first process will clean but not disinfect or dissolve any limescale in your toilet.

2 Squeeze the toilet cloth from the bucket of soapy water and

after a quick spray with all-purpose cleaner, wipe first the handle then the seat lid, both sides, and the seat, both sides.

3 With the seat lifted, wipe around the rim of the toilet, behind the seat and around the outside of the bowl.

4 The final clean to kill germs and leave the toilet fresh is a spray with the toilet magic. Spray it under the rim, then just leave it – do not flush.

One-off treatment

If like me your toilet-cleaning routine has previously involved chlorine bleach, then once the decision has been made to change cleaning methods the toilet will show up previously hidden secrets. You will probably notice that a grey mark will appear at the waterline, and there may be grey or green lines down the back of the toilet bowl. These are not new stains but simply old water marks and limescale deposits which had previously been 'bleached out' by the chlorine. They will harbour germs, are unsightly and can be corrosive if not treated. This tip is an expanded version of the weekly full clean.

1 Start by flushing the toilet. Sprinkle the washing soda around the bowl. (The soda will adhere if the toilet has just been flushed.) Take the toilet brush and work the soda around the rim of the bowl and into the water, scrubbing vigorously. Flush the toilet again. This first process will clean but not disinfect or dissolve any limescale in your toilet.

2 Squeeze the toilet cloth from the bucket of soapy water and wipe first the handle then the seat lid, both sides, and the seat, both sides.

3   With the seat lifted, wipe around the rim of the toilet, behind the seat and around the outside of the bowl.

4   To remove limescale and any water marks at the back of the toilet bowl where the water comes in, using the toilet brush in the water and four or five 'pumping' actions force the water back into the U-bend. By doing this you will lower the water level and expose the water mark, which will make it easy to treat.

5   Wring out your toilet cloth as dry as you can then dip the damp cloth into a small vessel containing the 2–3 tbsp citric acid crystals. Dab the crystals onto the water marks and limescale marks. The marks will probably feel rough to the touch. Pile as much citric acid on as you can and, depending on how severely marked the toilet is, leave for at least 20 minutes and up to an hour.

6   After leaving, and using your gloved finger, test to make sure the pan feels smooth. You will find that the citric acid crystals have dried on in a thin crust. Take the scourer and rub away at the crystals, paying particular attention to the waterline and limescale marks. Finish with a scrub around the bowl with the toilet brush and flush again. If you can still feel a rough limescale ridge, leave the citric acid crystals a little longer. It will do the job.

7   The final clean to kill germs and leave the toilet fresh is a spray with Nancy's Toilet Magic. Spray into the bowl and under the rim then just leave – do not flush.

I have to confess I had to do a huge toilet restoration job when I gave up on chlorine bleach. My downstairs toilet revealed a thick water mark along with rivers of limescale down the back of the bowl. The treatment took me two sessions – in the second one I left the citric acid on for well over an hour. Absolutely delighted with the results, but then alarmed that I had a hard lump of set citric acid crystals in the water at the bottom of the bowl – I had used around 4 tbsp. It felt like concrete, but before panic set in and 'him indoors' found out, I simply poured a kettle of boiling water down into the bowl, the crystals dissolved, the toilet flushed and all was good.

If you are not going to use Nancy's Toilet Magic daily, then the spray can seize up due to citric acid crystals re-forming inside the nozzle. After use, remove the spray attachment and rinse through with clean water then either replace or pop a screw top on the bottle until next time. If you find the spray has stuck, simply unscrew, pop into a jug and pour over very hot water. The nozzle will free up again as the citric acid crystals dissolve in the hot water.

To clean cloths that have been used for toilet cleaning, I tend to save them up and put them through a hot wash at the end of a house-cleaning session. The blue loo cloth I give a separate treatment (see pages 55–7) before putting it into the washing machine with the others. I have a separate old scratched Pyrex glass bowl just for this cloth.

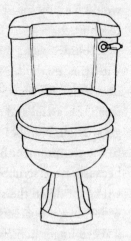

HOW TO CLEAN UNSIGHTLY BLACK MOULD AND STAINS FROM GROUTING AROUND TILES

Bathrooms and shower tiles are notorious for collecting black mould spots along the grouting and sealant which, if allowed to build up, can look unsightly, harbour germs and at worst start to smell. Mould build-up is caused because the atmosphere is damp and not well ventilated and can be particularly noticeable and problematic at the end of the winter when bathrooms have been used, condensation has built up and there has been little or no ventilation.

When the spring arrives, the days are warmer and longer, windows are opened and air is circulating, mould will not thrive, but it is necessary to clean away the unsightly build-up. I have to confess my solution to this annual problem used to be the chlorine bleach bottle! On with the rubber gloves, I would happily squirt it everywhere then take to it with an old toothbrush.

Looking back, there were at least three major problems with this method. Number one, I was breathing in all sorts of noxious fumes which I have now read are very potent. The smell was awful and probably wasn't doing me or the dogs any good at all. Number two, there was the damage I was causing to the environment by using large amounts of chlorine bleach, because after scrubbing away at my tiles I would rinse the whole lot down the sinks, into the drains and onward into our waterways. Apparently even small amounts of this toxic chemical can linger in our waterways for many years. Number three, bleach doesn't kill or prevent mould growth – it simply bleaches it and turns it white.

To kill mould, help prevent further outbreaks and clean away those unsightly black spots and patches took a little elbow grease, but the outcome was very satisfying.

How often do I need to clean away bathroom mould spots?

I consider this a once-a-year spring cleaning job.

You will need

glass bottle with spray attachment
150ml water
60ml white vinegar
40ml surgical spirit
20 drops organic lemon essential oil
2–3 tbsp bicarb
old toothbrush

First, I needed a solution to spray onto and into awkward areas – corners, nooks and crannies and hard-to-reach spots. In the spray bottle, mix the water, white vinegar, surgical spirit and lemon oil. The vinegar will kill the mould and help prevent further outbreaks and dissolve any limescale build-up on the grout and tiles, the surgical spirit will help to kill germs and bacteria and the lemon essential oil, as well as smelling gorgeous, has antiseptic and germ-killing properties of its own. Mixed together they make a great spray to use all around the bathroom, but particularly on the tiles to shine them up and get to work on that unsightly grouting.

I left the spray to soak into the grouting for 15 minutes or so, then wiped off as much of the mould as I could. I then dropped a couple of tablespoons of bicarb on the edge of my wash basin and shower tray. I dipped a dampened old toothbrush into the bicarb and gently scrubbed the remaining mould spots, being careful not to break the grouting or sealants.

The mould lifts easily, super-quickly and effectively. The job is super-satisfying and super-easy. A final wipe with a clean cloth, polish with a soft clean cloth and all is well!

If at first you don't succeed, don't be put off. There are those big problems – the heavily limescale-crusted tap, the thick green water mark or unsightly black mould stain – that call for stronger stuff. Make up a bottle of Nancy's Toilet Magic (see pages 194–5). She will bust her way through anything! Spray and leave on for a couple of hours, and even though it may take more than one application the citric acid will do the job. Wipe clean with a damp cloth to finish as citric acid can sometimes dry sticky. That's one of the reasons that the above method is better for an all-over treatment and to reserve Nancy's Toilet Magic for the more heavy-duty problem areas.

RUST SPOTS HAVE APPEARED
ON MY SHOWER HEAD!

I have a shower head that has a rubber rose, yet from time to time rust spots appear. I believe this is due to the fact that on the inside of the rose there must be metal parts that are rusting up from time to time and leaking onto the rose.

How often do I need to clean the rust spots on the shower head?

If rust spots appear on the rose of a shower head, treat them straight away.

You will need

200ml lemon juice or white vinegar
table salt

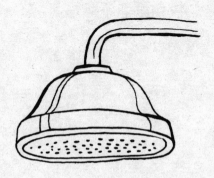

I am able to unscrew my shower head to make it easier to work with. Taking the shower head, I submerge it in a cup of lemon juice or white vinegar and leave it overnight. When I first tried this treatment, the next day the rust marks were still there, but once sprinkled with a little table salt I was able to rub over with my finger and the rust stains disappeared.

These stains reappear from time to time because I have not treated the cause, i.e., the rusting metal parts that I am unable to get to.

SPOT LIMESCALE REMOVER

When I refer to spot limescale, I mean those difficult patches of limescale that you may discover when a very slow and irregular drip from a bath or wash-hand basin tap has accumulated over time and formed a rough grey or green stain. Limescale is a problem in most hard water areas, and my sprays and cleaners all include natural acids which effectively dissolve it, preventing a build-up.

If you discover (often by feeling) a rough spot of limescale from a dripping tap, there will probably also be a ring of limescale around the plughole. I used to buy proprietary limescale removers which obviously treated the problem, but I needed to find something natural and safe for our waterways.

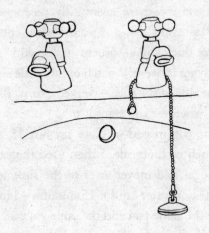

How often do I need to remove rough limescale spots?

Check below taps and around plugholes every two to three months.

You will need

half a cup of white vinegar
thick cotton reusable make-up remover pad

Understanding that both white vinegar (acetic acid) and lemons (citric acid) are great at dissolving limescale, the frustration was that if I tried to treat these difficult spots then the vinegar or lemon juice just ran down the sink. I needed a way to soak these spots for a length of time, allowing the natural acids to do their work.

The treatment for these awkwardly positioned limescale patches is to lay over them a vinegar-soaked cotton pad. The pads I have are thick and absorbent, and soaking one in white vinegar and laying it over the patch of limescale – even a patch halfway up the side of the bath – worked a treat. The wet cotton pad will stick wherever you want it to!

Leaving the cotton pad in place for just 15 minutes dissolved my patch of limescale. I then used the same pad and the same vinegar and moved over to the sink, left it on the spot under the hot water tap for 15 minutes – limescale gone! Finally, using the same pad and the same vinegar, I laid it over the plughole. You've guessed it – after 15 minutes the limescale was gone!

Limescale seems to go unnoticed, then one day a thick crust grabs the attention and may seem like a huge job calling for something stronger than a squirt of lemon juice or vinegar. Another frustration is that the limescale may be forming itself in a difficult-to-reach place. I have an old kitchen tap and around the seam about halfway down was a thick, crusty build-up. Limescale is corrosive, can harbour germs and is unsightly. I sprayed the build-up with my Nancy's Toilet Magic (which is a strong citric acid solution), then immediately tied a cotton ribbon around the limescale and sprayed again all over the ribbon too so that the whole lot was wetted. Leaving for 2 hours is sufficient to soften the toughest limescale so that it can be wiped away. Use a knife or coin to rub off any residual limescale in the seam of the metal where the tap joins the pipe or sink.

SLOW-FLOW SINK

The wash-hand basin in my bathroom is regularly on a go-slow, in that the water doesn't empty quickly and efficiently. This is probably due to soap scum or hair build-up in the waste pipe, and I used to buy chemical de-bung products which worked a treat, of course, probably because the caustic chemicals would just blast their way through any obstruction.

How often do I need to treat my slow-flow bathroom sink?

To correct a slow-flow sink treat as required, and to prevent blockages, treat once every three months.

You will need

150g washing soda
150ml boiling water
2–3 drops tea tree oil (optional,
    but will freshen the sink
    waste at the same time)
1 pint measuring jug
kettle of recently boiled water
    (later, to finish)

This treatment is best carried out before going to bed or when you know you will not use the sink for at least 8 hours.

Place the 150g washing soda into a Pyrex glass measuring jug, then pour over 150ml boiling water straight from the kettle. Stir to dissolve until you have a cloudy solution, then add the tea tree oil if using.

Pour the hot liquid directly down the plughole then put the plug in so that no further water is allowed to go down the sink, and leave for 8 hours.

The next morning bring a kettle of water to the boil, remove the plug in the sink and pour the boiled water straight down. Your sink will be clean, fresh, un-bunged and free-flowing.

GARDEN

This is in no way a gardening book, but the boundaries between home, kitchen and garden for me are fairly blurred. What is grown outside is brought into the kitchen, cooked and eaten or sometimes preserved. Living a clean and green life inside has to spill outside into the garden, too.

I have resisted using pesticides and insecticides for several years, and each season try different ways to control those pests that can devour the fruits of my labours literally overnight.

Followers too have inspired me to formulate eco-friendly sprays that will work without having to resort to chemical, harmful sprays which are bad for our own health and those of our pets, insects and birds.

MAKE YOUR OWN ECO-FRIENDLY PESTICIDE FOR GREENFLY, WHITEFLY AND APHIDS

It is widely known that bought pesticides are often toxic and, while effective in killing pests that chew away at your fruit and vegetables or strip the leaves from your prize roses and other flowers, they also cause great harm to bees, wild birds and ladybirds and other insects not considered by us to be pests!

I grow my own fruit and vegetables, and pest control is essential but doesn't have to be harmful to other insects and wildlife. Prevention is always better than cure, and healthy plants are less likely to suffer damaging attacks from predators and disease. Preparing soil with good compost before planting, regular watering and feeding where appropriate is essential and the gardener needs to be 'on it' at the first signs of unwanted visitors.

Rubbing the underside of cabbage leaves using just the fingers to destroy a cluster of eggs is far more effective than an overall toxic spray, which will probably not affect any unhatched eggs but will have destroyed the ladybirds which will feed on those eggs anyway, if given a chance. Nipping out the growing points of broad beans at the first sign of blackfly will eliminate the pests and encourage bushy growth of your plants.

Spraying greenfly which are clustering on your rosebuds with toxic chemicals will also kill the bees visiting a neighbouring bloom. If you have a heavy infestation of greenfly or whitefly on roses, then an eco-friendly spray can be made at home. It is essential that this is used in the evening after the sun has gone down, for two reasons. First, bees have gone to bed, so there is no fear of their being upset by the spray, and secondly, the home-made spray contains a little oil, which is necessary to help the spray stick to the leaves and not run straight off. If the sun is hot the oil will heat up and could scorch leaves.

How often do I need to use an eco-friendly pesticide?

Use at the first sign of unwanted visitors and repeat as necessary. Only apply in the evenings.

You will need

500ml water
1 tsp eco-friendly washing-up liquid/dish soap
2 tsp grapeseed oil
2–3 drops clove bud oil (insects hate it)
funnel
bottle with spray attachment

Using a funnel, measure 500ml water, 1 tsp eco-friendly washing-up liquid, 2 tsp grapeseed oil and 2–3 drops clove bud oil into a spray bottle. Shake well then spray over the offenders! This is a great spray to use on houseplants, too.

Clove bud oil is a fantastic insect deterrent and is used in many commercial insect repellents and weed killers.

NOTE: Always thoroughly wash any home-grown fruit and vegetables before using. A bowl of cold water with 1 tbsp table salt sprinkled in will wash fruit and veg as well as immediately killing any bugs. Your veggies will float to the top of the water and any hidden bugs will immediately sink to the bottom of the bowl.

DETER CATS AND DOGS FROM YOUR FAVOURITE PART OF THE GARDEN

I am guilty! During the dark, cold winter months I let my dogs out at night for their final toilet without taking too much notice about where they choose to relieve themselves. When the wind and blizzards blow, my dogs tend not to wander far and quickly do what has to be done, then run back into the warmth.

When the weather improves, the days get longer and my plants and flowers add beauty to my garden, I expect the dog to no longer urinate near the house or against my favourite planter or tree. It is unfair on the dog if I begin to chastise him when, for the best part of the last six months, he has been able to please himself. Instead, I prefer to arrange for the chosen place to become off-putting and to no longer be the best-smelling toilet spot around.

How often do I need to deter my pet from a favourite garden toilet?

Every day for a week or until the habit is broken.

You will need

200ml water
50ml white vinegar
30 drops organic peppermint oil (or lemon/orange essential oil)
bottle with spray attachment

Mix the ingredients together into a spray bottle, then to break your dog or cat's habit of using the wrong place for their toilet, pop out daily to spray their favourite areas. Dogs will want to urinate first thing in the morning and straight after food. If you can get there first and while the deterrent spray is fresh, still wet and at its most strong smelling, then the dog will avoid the scent left by the peppermint and vinegar. Vinegar will help to destroy previous scents and odours and the essential oil will permeate the area. Dogs and cats dislike the smell of peppermint and citrus.

Continue to spray every day – more often if the weather is wet. In a day or two your dog will find a new toilet.

NOTE: Do not spray directly onto plants as vinegar can kill foliage. If the dog is visiting a favourite plant or bush, spray instead an imaginary border around the plant on the ground – this should deter them.
Never spray on or near your pets.

FIELD MICE IN THE GREENHOUSE OR GARDEN SHED

There is evidence of mice in your shed or greenhouse if there are droppings or your plants and seed packets have been chewed. Chances are it is a little field mouse who has found a handy food supply. Rather than set a trap or leave poison (which is also poisonous to other animals), I prefer to deter the little chap.

How often do I need to deter field mice from the greenhouse or shed?

At first sign of mouse droppings, or if you detect someone small is eating your plants and seeds.

You will need

200ml water
40 drops organic peppermint
    essential oil
bottle with spray attachment

Always keep seeds in a metal box, and don't leave any food-stuffs lying around. If you can see where the mouse is entering, then fill in the hole. Mice are so tiny it is likely you have no idea where his door is – instead spray the peppermint spray liberally all along the base of your shed or greenhouse. Repeat daily and your mouse will find another restaurant with better air conditioning.

RHUBARB AND NETTLE BUG FIXES
FOR VEG, PLANTS AND FLOWERS

Being a keen gardener, composting, hand-weeding, mulching and generally being vigilant around my flowers, fruit and vegetables goes a long way to keeping them in the best of health. However, even the keenest eyes can overlook bugs and pests, and if left untreated these can soon damage your favourite roses, shrubs and veggies.

I have spent time reading and trying various natural bug treatments over the past two years. Some potions had no effect whatsoever and after much trying and failing, trying and failing, I consider the following two recipes to be effective. The first uses rhubarb leaves, which are high in oxalic acid and which pests hate. I have further enhanced the mix with the addition of clove bud oil. Clove bud oil contains eugenol which repels insects and helps to control fungal disease, and indeed I found this to be the case when some of my rose leaves were covered in a white powdery mildew – the fungus disappeared after just one spray with this, but for those of you without a ready supply of rhubarb leaves, I have an alternative version (see pages 223–6). The second mix takes over a week to make and uses nettles with the addition of clove bud oil. This mix I will use on my edible plants and vegetables – a great plant food, too.

As with any plant sprays, always keep away from children and pets.

How often do I need to use a bug fix?

At the first sign of greenfly, whitefly or aphids (May or June in the UK).

You will need

FOR THE RHUBARB SPRAY

500g rhubarb leaves (not the stalks – have them in a pie)

1 litre water

1–2 drops eco-friendly washing-up liquid/dish soap

20 drops clove bud oil

large saucepan with lid

scissors

litre bottle with spray attachment

FOR THE NETTLE SPRAY

60g nettles – leaves and stalks

600ml cold water

1–2 drops eco-friendly washing-up
   liquid/dish soap

6 drops clove bud oil

rubber gloves

scissors

old saucepan or casserole pan with lid

litre bottle with spray attachment

Rhubarb spray for decorative garden plants and flowers
Makes approximately 1 litre. Cut up the leaves into shreds with
scissors and pop them in a large saucepan. Pour over 1 litre of
cold water then bring to the boil and simmer with a tight-
fitting lid for 30 minutes. Leave to cool in the pan then strain
(I used a tea strainer) into a large spray bottle.

Add 1–2 drops eco-friendly washing-up liquid, then the
clove bud oil. The eco-friendly washing-up liquid will help to
emulsify the oil.

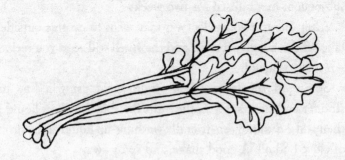

Shake well before use then spray onto blackfly, whitefly and greenfly. I followed up with a second and even third daily spray on huge infestations of blackfly. The spray contains oxalic acid which is a poison, and for that reason I will not be using it on my edibles – fruit, vegetables, and so on.

For those readers who don't grow rhubarb, ask at your local fruit and veg shop, market stall or allotment. The leaves are removed before selling because they are large and inedible – they will be happy for you to take the leaves off their hands.

Add the boiled leaves to the compost heap. The oxalic acid breaks down as it decomposes and the resulting compost is suitable for widespread use.

Nettle spray for use on edible plants

Makes approximately 500ml. Wearing gloves, cut your nettles with scissors then cut into 2–3-inch (5–7cm) lengths and pop into a roomy pan or old casserole pan with a lid. Pour over 600ml cold water, give it a stir and push the nettles into the water, pop the lid on and leave outside and forget about it for at least a week – stirring maybe once or twice during that time. I left mine only six days because I was impatient, though my subsequent mix infused for two weeks.

After one to two weeks (you may want to do this outside), take off the lid, give it a stir and the smell will send you reeling – it really is awful!

Strain off the leaves, then strain again using a fine tea strainer and fill a spray bottle with the foul-smelling liquid. I then add 2 drops of eco-friendly washing-up liquid and 6 drops of clove bud oil. A good shake, and spray away.

I use this spray on my vegetables as it not only kills aphids, but the clove bud oil will deter insects, the washing-up liquid helps it to stick to the leaves and not run straight off and the foul-smelling nettle water is adored by plants and will give them a welcome liquid feed.

I would not harvest any vegetables until two days after spraying and, as always, wash well. Add the nettle leaves to the compost heap.

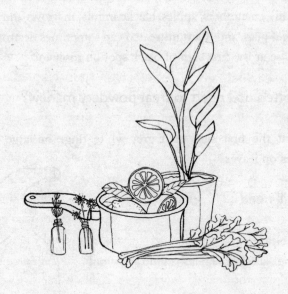

POWDERY MILDEW ON ROSES AND EDIBLE PLANTS

Powdery mildew is easy to detect and actually looks as though the leaves of your plants have been sprayed pale grey. Powdery mildew is a fungus and thrives in cool, damp conditions. It can be destructive, too, and left untreated will cause leaves to shrivel and die. Rose leaves become distorted and if the fungus is allowed to attack the flower buds it can prevent them from opening. Powdery mildew also adores the leaves of courgettes (zucchini), cucumbers, apples, blackcurrants, marrows and peas and sweet peas, and if left untreated can sometimes destroy the plant. Use at the first sign of black spot on roses too.

How often do I need to treat powdery mildew?

Spray at the first sign of a grey-white tinge or large grey blotches on leaves.

You will need

1 tsp bicarb
3 drops eco-friendly washing-up liquid/dish soap
350ml water (100ml warm and 250ml cold)
500ml bottle with spray attachment

Quick and easy to mix. Measure the bicarb straight into a spray bottle, then add about 100ml warm water. Shake the bottle to help mix the ingredients, then add the washing-up liquid and the rest of the water. Shake and it is ready for use.

I understand from further reading that the bicarb solution creates an alkaline environment on the leaf which makes it difficult for the powdery mildew fungus to survive and thrive.

Strong, healthy, well-watered plants will often resist the fungus but at first signs of an attack spray well in the evening when the weather is still. Repeat every week, as necessary.

I have used both bicarb spray and my nettle spray (see pages 223–7) and both have been effective. There are sprays on the market that will do the job too, but beware: there are a number which are, it is stated, harmful to aquatic life.

PEST CONTROL – SLUGS AND SNAILS

Slugs and snails can destroy a treasured row of lettuce plants and many other green-leaved veggies, and I once had a bed of marigolds nibbled overnight, never to recover. Slugs and snails will make an appearance when the weather is warm and damp. They will slither along happily over damp soil and grass and love night-time feasting.

There are many slug pellets on the market which attract gastropods – they will eat them and then they die. Unfortunately, birds, frogs, toads and hedgehogs that then go on to eat these poisoned pests will perish too. Much more eco-friendly to deter the slimy characters, and this can be done effectively and at minimal cost.

How often do I need to use pest control for slugs and snails?

At the first signs of slug or snail damage to flowers or vegetables.

You will need

eggshells
table salt

Whenever you use an egg, get into the habit of rinsing the eggshell under the tap, removing the slimy membrane then leaving it to dry and placing it in a bowl. Once a collection of six or seven shells has been accumulated, simply crush them with your hands to a fine crumb. Stir through half a teaspoon of table salt then sprinkle along your row of veggies and plants.

Don't go too close to the plants with the crumb because although plants can tolerate an amount of salt, too much can be poisonous.

Slugs and snails will stay well clear – their slimy composition finds it impossible to navigate a crazy-paving path of dry eggshells, and the coating of salt will create an immediate sting and they will slide away as the salt can be fatal.

As with slug pellets, applying the treatment straight after a downpour of rain is better than before a shower.

PLANT FOOD FOR YOUR CUT FLOWERS

I have two small vases, and cut a few bits from the garden whatever the season. In springtime, there may be a handful of primroses or daffodils (the mini ones); in the summer, sweet peas or anything that takes my fancy, and the autumn and winter can just be a bunch of berries or evergreens. Prolonging their life from four to five days to up to a week, or even ten days, can be achieved with this simple flower food.

How often do I need to add cut flower food?

Use to prolong the life of your garden cut flowers or bought flowers without having to resort to a plastic sachet, or, as is well documented, household chlorine bleach. Bleach is banned from my eco-friendly life.

You will need

1 heaped tsp sugar
1–2 tsp white vinegar
hot water
cold water
500ml vase – double or treble the
    quantities of sugar and vinegar
    for larger vases

Add a teaspoon of sugar to a clean vase (500ml capacity), then pour over a few tablespoons of hot water (not boiling water because you could crack your best antique cut-glass vase!) and swirl around until the sugar dissolves and the water is clear. If the sugar is added to the vase and topped off with cold water, then the sugar will sit at the bottom of the vase, looking unsightly in a clear vase, and may not do its job.

Once the sugar is dissolved, add the white vinegar and top up with cold water. I have found that tender-stemmed flowers such as sweet peas require only 1 tsp vinegar. Add your freshly cut flowers and enjoy for up to 50% longer. When I ran an experiment using two vases – one with flower food and one with just water – my garden flowers with the food lasted a week, whereas the vase with plain water lasted four days.

The sugar feeds the flowers and the white vinegar is a clear acidifier to prevent any bacteria build-up in the water. The mix does not cloud the water so is perfect for clear glass vases.

Remember to top up the water each day as cut flowers can be very thirsty.

WEED CONTROL FOR PATIOS, PATHS AND PAVERS

There are many weed killer products on the market, and after years of widespread use, researchers are uncovering evidence that they are potentially toxic to human cells as they are leaving residues in food and water. There is plenty to read on the subject, including danger to pets and children, and this has been enough to motivate me to try natural alternatives.

Hand-weeding, whilst it may be my preferred method and can be easy when the weather conditions are damp and the weeds are easily lifted, is also time-consuming, back-breaking and there are some very difficult to get at areas where weeds just cannot be lifted. Those difficult weeds that tuck themselves into cracks between pavers and on paths and block paving can make hand-weeding virtually impossible.

When looking for an effective natural spot weed control it doesn't get any easier than salt and water!

How often do I need to treat the weeds on the patio, path or pavers?

As required, but especially during the growing months of May and June.

You will need

table salt
kettle of boiling water

Choose a time when the weather forecast is dry, and pour a thin stream of boiling water over your weeds then immediately follow up with a direct sprinkle of table salt. After four to five days the weeds will have shrivelled and died back, with no toxic chemicals being washed into waterways via the soil. When considering how much salt to apply, simply think about the size of the problem – a huge daisy or dandelion (which will have a sizable carrot-shaped root) will need a good teaspoon of salt, whereas a tuft of wild grass will require much less.

I treated the weeds between pavers on my patio and block paving, and even though the weather turned and the treatment suffered two days of rain, the weeds still died within five days – and did not reappear for a whole season. Destroy any weeds with this, but remember, it will kill your precious plants, too, so hand-weeding is necessary on flower beds and vegetable plots.

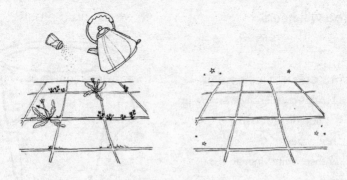

GIVE NEW LIFE TO THAT NEGLECTED WOODEN GARDEN SEAT

Tired, neglected wooden garden furniture can be cleaned and treated for a fraction of the cost of commercial treatments. Mixing a few cupboard ingredients and a little time will give that seat renewed presence in your garden.

When you have precious new garden furniture, you may want to follow the manufacturer's instructions and buy the recommended teak oil or special protection, but for that garden seat left to the elements, green with algae and splattered with bird droppings, here is an alternative. I also used this method to revamp my garden shed.

How often do I need to treat wooden garden furniture?

Once a year.

You will need

TO CLEAN
1 tbsp eco-friendly washing-up
    liquid/dish soap
hot water
3 tbsp white vinegar

5 drops tea tree oil

bucket and scrubbing brush

TO TREAT

130ml grapeseed oil (or olive, sunflower, vegetable oil)

50ml white vinegar

½ tsp brown food colour gel

2–3 drops eco-friendly washing-up liquid/dish
    soap

glass jar with screw top

rubber gloves

soft brush or cloth to apply

Start by cleaning the wood of all the grime. A bucket of hot soapy water with vinegar and tea tree oil added will not only clean but will kill any algae and quickly dissolve the bird droppings and other garden debris. Allow the seat or item to dry completely – a windy, sunny day is perfect for this.

To mix the treatment, measure the ingredients into a jar. The oil, vinegar and food colour will not readily mix, but adding a few drops of eco-friendly washing-up liquid, screwing on the top tightly then giving it a good shake will emulsify the contents to a thick brown liquid.

Then, using gloved hands, apply the treatment with a brush or soft cloth, but either way work it into the wood. Leave to dry completely then apply a second coat. The treatment soaks well in helping to waterproof, stain and replenish the wood.

PERSONAL

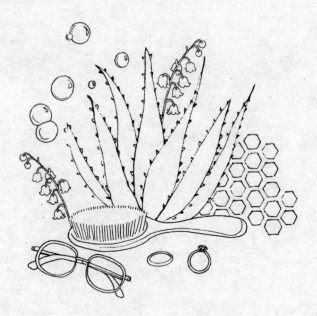

have included what can best be described as my 'personal' section, because these tips fall outside of household cleaning. Without delving into the huge health and beauty arena, there are a few tips that I have found useful and that have made me quite proud. Following a little research, reading, practising and using, here are some great little tips and recipes that work and will save money.

LIP BALM, SORE SKIN AND DRY SKIN SOFTENER

I think I have had a jar of petroleum jelly in the cupboard for as long as I can remember. An affordable go-to product for sore lips, chapped legs, dry skin and many a child's ailment when there was nothing else to hand.

I always considered it simple, harmless and sustainable until I started to do some reading. I know, of course, that it is derived from refining oil, and is therefore a by-product of the oil industry.

I decided to make a lip balm and sore skin comforter that is natural.

It is quick and easy to make, and can be used just as soon as the liquid sets. It is handy to have small glass pots with screw tops that can be popped into a handbag or pocket. Attractive little screw-top glass jars make great gifts. I gave each of my granddaughters a pot and they loved it.

You will need

30g coconut oil
15g beeswax pellets
25ml grapeseed or olive oil
1–2 drops peppermint extract (optional)

Place all the ingredients in a small heatproof bowl, then pop over a pan of recently boiled water. Turn off the heat to the pan and leave the contents to melt slowly. The coconut oil will melt first, and once the beeswax has liquefied, you will have a clear liquid.

Stir well then transfer to small glass jars and leave to set.

This natural, soothing balm will prevent sore lips, comfort your sore nose and does a fantastic job on dry skin on feet! A little goes a long way. For those with sensitive skin or skin conditions, I would recommend doing a patch test first.

CLEANING GOLD JEWELLERY ITEMS AND RINGS WITH STONES

I have a number of treasures! I wear my wedding ring all the time, but my engagement ring and eternity ring I wear only when I am not in the kitchen. When I examine them closely I can see them looking dull and lacking in lustre. This can be due to soap (when washing my hands) and hand cream.

Rather than buy jewellery dips and chemical-impregnated cloths, it is easy to clean jewellery naturally.

How often do I need to clean my gold jewellery?

I tend to give my engagement ring and eternity ring a quick clean most times I wear them, which is not every day.

You will need

warm water
eco-friendly washing-up liquid/dish soap
small bowl
small, soft brush – I use a short-haired make-up brush or a soft toothbrush
soft, clean polishing cloth

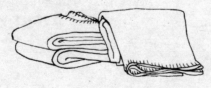

When cleaning my rings, I pour the warm water into a bowl first before adding the washing-up liquid to avoid creating suds. Drop the rings into the solution and leave to soak for 15 minutes.

> NOTE: Avoid using very hot water as it could have an adverse effect on precious stones. Pearls, for example, are very delicate and very hot water can damage them.

After the soak, take the soft brush and gently massage around the tiny areas where grease and grime could have built up. The soak will have softened any dirt and it will remove easily. Finally, take the polishing cloth and dry around the ring or chain then leave in an airy place to dry off completely.

My grandmother used to have a saying: 'Jewellery should always be last on and first off.' Avoid applying make-up, hairspray, lotions or perfumes once your jewellery is on – particularly earrings – in order to keep it looking gorgeous.

MY PEARL NECKLACE

Just a note on my pearl necklace. Many followers comment that I wear a string of pearls most of the time – hilarious – even when cleaning the toilet!

I adore my pearl necklace. Routine care is simply a polish with a dry cloth. While it keeps the pearls hydrated, body oil can weaken the thread, so a check once a year or so with the jeweller is recommended to make sure all is well. This is not a throwaway comment – my string of pearls did snap next to the fastener because the silk thread had become weak. A string of pearls should be knotted between each pearl so that the whole string is not lost if the thread breaks.

Importantly, never submerge a string of pearls in water as you would for a silver or gold necklace as this can weaken the silk thread, and equally, never use an ultrasonic cleaner as this can damage the pearls themselves.

If you want your string of pearls to live a long and happy life, and perhaps be handed down the generations, did you know that the best care for pearls is to wear them? Pearls are prone to scratches and should always be stored flat. Pearls also like a moist environment, so wearing them keeps them from drying out.

How often do I need to check the thread on my pearls?

Check briefly whenever taking them on and off. I clean mine maybe every three months and have an annual check with a jeweller.

You will need

warm water
few drops eco-friendly washing-up liquid/dish soap
dry cloth

Pearls, like other gemstones are natural and so should always be cleaned and cared for naturally. Just a soft cleaning cloth dipped in a warm solution of water and washing-up liquid and wiped over the pearls is sufficient to remove any grease or dirt. Let them air-dry before placing them back into a box stored flat, rather than hanging, to prevent the thread or threads from stretching.

CLEANING OF DENTAL RETAINERS, MOUTH GUARDS AND DENTURES

Many people wear dental retainers, mouth guards and dentures, and many use proprietary cleaning products containing chemicals that are strong-tasting, and there are some that are considered harmful. I decided to make my own.

I had a dental retainer that had to be worn from twenty to twenty-two hours a day, and apart from the fact that the cleaning product recommended was sold in sealed single-use plastic packets, there was a significant monthly cost involved and also a number of chemical additions. I remember replacing my retainer after cleaning and rinsing and tasting that distinct 'swimming pool chlorine' taste, which prompted me to read the ingredients list. No surprise to find that the chemical used to clean swimming pools was included in the ingredients.

After reading around the subject and taking on board the words of professionals in the field, I decided to make my own. Bicarb and white vinegar are easy, cheap and effective ways to disinfect and clean dentures, retainers and mouth guards naturally. Bicarb is a safe, all-purpose cleaner and will whiten retainers that have yellowed. Bicarb can control bacteria without adding harsh chemicals. White vinegar is a natural disinfectant that will neutralize odours and destroy any residues. The acid in the vinegar will dissolve tartar that can build up on the denture or retainer.

How often do I need to clean my dental retainer or dentures?

Daily clean – make the solution once a week.

You will need

100ml white vinegar
300ml cooled boiled water
1 tsp bicarb per clean
few drops peppermint extract (optional)
pretty storage bottle – about 500ml
small glass jar with a screw top

Place the vinegar and water in a pretty storage bottle and keep this on your bathroom shelf – add a few drops of peppermint extract if you want to improve the taste. After brushing the retainer lightly with a soft toothbrush dipped in bicarb (refrain from using toothpaste to clean retainers – I've read it is too abrasive) rinse it then pop it into the small jar with a screw top, add enough vinegar and water solution to cover, then replace the lid and give the jar a shake.

Leave for 15–20 minutes, rinse and pop the retainer back into the mouth. Discard the cleaning fluid down the sink – no worries about pollution.

No need for single-use packaging, goodness-knows-what chemicals, and the job is done cheaply and perfectly.

If you find yourself out of toothpaste, bicarb mixed to a paste with water, a pinch of salt and a drop of peppermint extract makes an excellent standby. Maybe not a good idea for small children as they often eat most of their toothpaste and swallowing too much bicarb isn't very good for you.

BATH AND SHOWER GEL

This is one of my favourite home-made recipes! Inexpensive, does the job, no extra plastic or synthetic chemicals and the perfume choice is up to you, but I have fallen for lily of the valley – it is unbelievable.

I wanted my 'natural' bath and shower gel to make my skin feel soft, I wanted it to be harmless to the waterways, I wanted perfume and I wanted a thick non-coloured cream.

I considered Castile soap would be my basic ingredient. Castile soap is a surfactant-free natural soap base made from organic oils of coconut and sunflower. It will not dry out the skin and can be used as a shower gel, shampoo and handwash. Surfactants, as I understand it, are those chemicals used in many skin products, shampoos and detergents that help to emulsify the ingredients – many of which are toxic to humans and the environment.

I then went on to add vegetable glycerine, which mixed in nicely and would soften my skin, as would the aloe vera gel. I added in the lily of the valley oil for fragrance and I had the beginnings of a fabulous shower gel – but alas, the mixture was too thin.

I had a think about thickeners I use routinely in cooking and baking, and considered that if they are safe to eat they will be safe to use on the skin. I did some further reading around cornflour and xanthan gum, only to discover that xanthan gum is widely used in organic skincare products and is thought to have some hydrating benefits for the skin. Cornflour, too, I read is widely used in bath bombs and cosmetics as it contains a reasonable amount of protein that helps boost collagen and prevents the signs of skin ageing – *and I'm up for that!* Simply pour 1–2 tbsp under running water in the bath, or use as you would a commercial shower gel. If you like a few bubbles add a few drops of eco-friendly washing up liquid to the recipe.

You will need

12g cornflour (3 tsp)
100ml cold water
60ml Castile soap
20ml vegetable glycerine
10ml aloe vera gel
10 drops organic lily of the valley essential oil (or your favourite fragrance)
¼ tsp xanthan gum
small saucepan

small whisk
small funnel
250–300ml decorative glass bottle or pump dispenser

To make the bath or shower gel, measure the cornflour into a small saucepan then add the cold water little by little, stirring well with the small whisk until there are no lumps. Add in the Castile soap, vegetable glycerine, essential oil fragrance and aloe vera gel. Place the pan over a low heat and keep stirring until the mixture starts to bubble and thicken and turns a translucent colour.

Take off the heat and sprinkle over the xanthan gum and keep stirring. Stir for several minutes and you will see the gel will colour white, thicken considerably and smell divine.

I save plastic shower gel bottles and, using a plastic funnel, transfer the thick gel. Then it is easy to dispense just a measured amount onto a sponge or shower puff.

PERFUMED AND COLOURED BATH SALTS

I recall as a child bath time was just a once-a-week event. Sunday night was for hair-washing and a bath. There was no bubble bath, just a sprinkling of washing soda in the water to soften it enough so that the soap could make a lather. One Christmas I remember being gifted a glass jar of pink bath crystals, which I suspect would have been simply either washing soda or Epsom salts. I used them sparingly because they were slightly perfumed and I thought they were very luxurious.

I love a good soak in the bath – it is relaxing, warming and comforting. I like to add relaxing bath salts or bubble bath, too. I always thought bubble bath was basically liquid soap. As with many other products, when I read the label on the back of the bottle and investigated thoroughly, I realized I was quite wrong. The brands I used contained quite a hefty dose of chemicals which apart from being bad for the environment, were probably not doing my skin a lot of good either. My other consideration was that it is always sold in plastic bottles, packaged attractively and promising a soothing, comforting, relaxing experience. Lots of lovely colours to choose from, too. I decided to make my own, much cheaper, using natural ingredients and no synthetic chemicals.

You will need

400g Epsom salts

50g bicarb

10–15 drops organic essential oil (e.g., orange, lily of the valley, grapefruit)

4–6 drops natural food or soap colour (optional)

500g decorative jar

FOR COLOURED, SCENTED SALTS Measure the Epsom salts into a large plastic box that has a well-fitting lid. Add the food or soap colour of choice then spoon over the bicarb. Add the drops of essential oil fragrance of choice directly onto the bicarb, then put the lid on the box and give everything a good shake. I found that the bicarb absorbs the perfumed oil, preventing it from clumping, and then infuses the rest of the salts. Transfer the contents into your favourite jar, decorate with a piece of coloured ribbon and you have an inexpensive delightful gift for yourself or a friend.

Add 3–4 tbsp to the bath as the hot tap is running and the salts and soda will readily dissolve, soften the water, soothe the skin, soften rough, dry skin, reduce soreness and pain and the perfume is gorgeous.

The theory is that when you soak in an Epsom salts bath the salts and the warm water can help relax muscles and loosen stiff joints. My grandmother always used Epsom salts as a home treatment for arthritis pain and swelling. If I want a few bubbles, too, I add a squirt of my bath and shower gel (see pages 250–2).

I must just tell you this! As I have mentioned already, I now buy my main cleaning staples such as vinegar, bicarb, citric acid and surgical spirit in bulk because I know I will use them up, it is cheaper in the long run to buy this way and I consume less plastic packaging. I needed Epsom salts to work on the recipe ideas I had in mind for this tip, so quickly clicked 'buy now', as you do, without reading the small print. A huge box arrived some days later, and feeling puzzled as to what it could be I opened the package to discover a 10kg tub of Epsom salts! Needless to say I now have sufficient base ingredient for bath salts for me and my family. There will be pretty jars containing scented crystals being given as gifts for Christmas – not just this year but for many years to come!

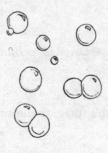

CLEAN GLASSES AND SUNGLASSES

There are many glasses and sunglasses cleaners on the market and a number of single-use options which – apart from the extra packaging involved – as with any single-use wipes, are bad for the environment. They find themselves into waterways and sewers as people flush single-use items down the toilet often without thinking.

You will need

150ml water

60ml white vinegar

40ml surgical spirit

few drops organic essential oil for perfume (optional) – I use lily of the valley

small plastic funnel

small glass bottle with a spray attachment (a handbag-size bottle is useful, too)

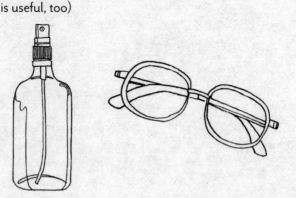

I find a small plastic funnel makes the measuring and mixing so much quicker and avoids any spills. Just add the measured amounts to a small spray bottle. A quick shake, and it is good to go. A handy pocket-sized bottle for holidays and 'on the move' is a must.

Glasses and sunglasses can get oily from handling, and grease from make-up and sun creams create smears and marks, too. Make up this fantastic spray, then a quick squirt and polish with a soft cloth and you'll be dazzling again.

CLEAN HAIRBRUSHES AND COMBS

Brushes and combs tend to be overlooked when it comes to cleaning until you take a look one day to see your comb's teeth have a coating of grey scum, your brush bristles are the same and there is a matting of hair stuck around the bristles.

How often do I need to clean my hairbrush and comb?

Once a month.

You will need

> squirt of eco-friendly washing-up liquid/dish soap
> surgical spirit (if there have been head lice)
> jug

Time for action. I find it easier to clean either a brush and a comb or two brushes together at the same time. Rub one against the other to loosen hair and pull this off and discard. Once you have removed the loose hair, simply squirt about a tablespoon of washing-up liquid into a tall jug and pour on hot water. Submerge the comb and brush and leave for at least an hour.

Plastic heads on brushes will tend to float, so weigh it down with a metal kitchen utensil. After an hour, rub the two brushes together in the water and they will become squeaky clean.

Washing brushes regularly also helps to prevent static electricity, which is a nuisance when trying to style hair. If you do find a static problem, then a quick fix is just a fine spray of water onto the brush or comb.

If there has been an infestation of head lice in the family, then washing in this way will not be enough. Soaking brushes and combs in surgical spirit will kill any lice. I would soak the items in a shallow bowl, in order to use less surgical spirit.

HANDY HAND SANITIZER

Making my own natural hand sanitizer seemed a little pointless when I considered the fact that it is not expensive to buy, is used infrequently and there are plenty of other eco-friendly green products that I could be concentrating on.

However, panic struck just before I sat down to write this book. The coronavirus was the top news story every day, and suddenly people all around the world were panic buying foods, toiletries and in particular hand-sanitizing gels. The public health warnings were to wash hands regularly with soap and water and to use sanitizing gel. Trouble was, all sanitizing gel products quickly sold out.

Government health departments warned against home-made gel because it probably wasn't strong enough to kill the virus, but I felt following further reading that rather than having nothing at all, a home-made option was preferable, provided it had an alcohol 'bug killing' concentration of at least 60%. At the time of writing we were in the middle of the coronavirus pandemic, and many people made their own sanitizers as they were in such short supply in the shops and supermarkets. As with any home-made personal product, it is recommended that it is patch-tested and only ever used on the hands, not the face or anywhere more sensitive.

How often do I need to use hand sanitizer?

Ever been out and about and felt maybe your hands could do with a wash before eating or drinking? Maybe you've been travelling on public transport and are worried about who has been where! Maybe there's a bug going around, and you want to do everything you can to keep it at bay. Even worse, you have visited a public toilet only to find there are no suitable hand-washing and -drying facilities. Having a bottle of hand sanitizer in your bag or car may just save the day.

You will need

FOR 100ML

35ml aloe vera gel

65ml surgical spirit (rubbing alcohol – 95% concentration)

2–3 drops organic lemon essential oil

small bowl or jar

mini whisk

funnel

2 used and cleaned glass cosmetic pump action bottles
   (2 x 50ml approx)

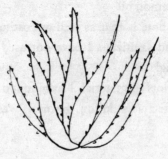

The sanitizer is easy to make, but I realized after one spoilt batch that it has to be mixed in a certain way. First, measure the aloe vera gel (for softness to the skin) into a small bowl or jar, then use a mini whisk to give it a good beating. Then add the alcohol (surgical spirit or rubbing alcohol) which will kill the bugs. Most importantly, add the alcohol little by little, whisking well between each addition. If the alcohol is added too quickly the solution separates and the aloe vera gel floats around in lumps. Finally add 2–3 drops lemon essential oil – this adds a fresh fragrance to the sanitizer and also has antiseptic properties of its own.

If your sanitizer does split and separate, it can be rescued. A drop of eco-friendly washing-up liquid added and a blitz with a hand blender will emulsify the liquid.

Use a funnel to pour the cloudy liquid into the two clean cosmetic pump spray bottles and it is ready for use.

It is worth noting that if the rubbing alcohol or surgical spirit you buy is less than 95% concentration, you may want to adjust your ingredients as follows:

Alcohol strength 90% – 70ml alcohol plus 30ml aloe vera gel and 2–3 drops lemon oil

Alcohol strength 80% – 75ml alcohol plus 25ml aloe vera gel and 2–3 drops lemon oil

A final little note is that as well as costing much less than commercial hand sanitizers, I have not used any unnecessary plastic packaging!

Having read lots of material, I have found it is evident that nothing is as effective at killing germs as washing hands with soap and water.

HOW TO CLEAN

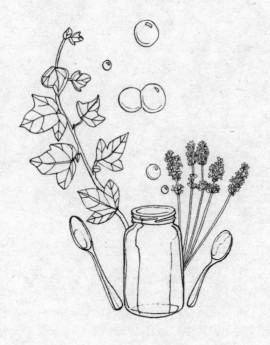

have included this section for those readers who need a little direction or step-by-step guidance when it comes to cleaning a house.

If a house is to be a home, then family and visitors should not feel afraid to set foot in the place for fear of making a mess. The house should be comfortable, cheery, welcoming and clean. I am not a person who is forever cleaning the house, but equally my house has to feel and smell clean. When I say smell clean I don't mean it smells of perfume or products – on the contrary, it smells fresh and neutral as opposed to smelling dirty, doggy, fusty or stale.

I find it useful to have a little timetable to use as a guide – and I say guide – don't be a slave to housework, but don't let things get so bad that they turn into huge tasks. Cleaning has to be done whatever your circumstances. Cleaning when you live alone is less demanding than when there is a young family with resulting spills and accidents, an older family with teen-agers leaving a trail of destruction everywhere they go and now in my case just two adults, but then two dogs who create dirt without realizing – they neither know nor care whether their feet are muddy or clean!

I will start with my once- or twice-a-year jobs which I usually begin in the springtime when the days get longer and warmer. Doors and windows can be opened, the heating is not on as often, fires are turned off and the sun shines through the grubby windows showing up all sorts of winter dust and grime. However, don't be overwhelmed into thinking that a full spring clean has to be done on one day. My plan is usually to tackle one room at a time, and that one room becomes part of a rolling weekly programme. Whether your house has two, three, four or fourteen rooms, cleaning one room at a time thoroughly will give the best results rather than trying to do a little bit of a clean in every room without ever bottoming out and leaving no stone unturned.

Start at the top, and by that I mean upstairs, and within that upstairs room start at the ceiling and work down. Dust and dirt will fall to the floor, so the floors should always be the last to clean.

Alternatively, you may want to start with the room that is the most used and seemingly the dirtiest, and this is often the kitchen. Same rules apply – start at the top, above eye level, and don't forget the tops of cupboards, light fittings and shelves that always attract a layer of dusty grease. A spray with the all-purpose cleaner and a damp cloth will cut through it in a jiffy. Work your way down, finishing with the floor.

Kitchen cupboards also need a periodic clear-out and clean, and again it doesn't have to be done all in a day. My days for this kind of task involve rain outside, radio on full blast, meal out of the freezer so that I don't have to cook. I am happy to create chaos getting everything out, dancing, singing, washing everything down and putting things away again in an orderly fashion. So satisfying.

Once the spring clean or deep clean is complete, then there

are those jobs that probably need attending to every six months, then every month, every week and every day. A simple routine will keep your cleaning structured and effective – so here goes . . .

There will be those jobs that you love and those jobs that are creatively avoided at all costs. For example, I have absolutely no problem keeping my oven clean – I enjoy the ease of the green clean. Yet cleaning windows, that is another story, and if there is rain forecast over the next ten days then that is a good enough excuse to put it off for a little longer, although I always get there eventually. Popping on the radio as I work away really helps.

ONCE- OR TWICE-A-YEAR DEEP CLEAN

Feather duster to ceilings and walls to remove cobwebs.

Wipe or wash light shades and fittings – if you have glass ceiling ornaments or chandeliers, then a pair of cotton gloves will make cleaning quick and easy – much better than a duster.

Vacuum or brush pelmets and tops of curtains – don't be tempted to take a damp cloth to dusty soft furnishings as the dirt will lodge into the fabric.

Clean the inside of windows using warm water and a vinegar spray which will cut through the greasy film that forms on the inside (see pages 134–6).

Dust the tops of picture frames, doors, wardrobes and mirrors.

Pull out furniture items from their place and clean behind, dusting skirting boards and vacuuming carpets and floors. If you fancy having a change around at the same time, see the tip about removing dints from your carpet (see pages 165–6).

Tip chairs forward to clean the underneath of any cobwebs and dust, particularly if you have furniture with legs.

Take cushions from chairs and vacuum soft furnishings.

Polish wood furniture (see pages 146–8).

I use a soft clothes brush to brush lampshades – they collect lots of dust!

Clean any copper, brass or silver items (see pages 123–6 for copper, 137–45 for brass and silver).

Wash any ornaments, fruit bowls, and so on – ornaments collect dust in creases which will wash off easily but will not come off by dusting alone.

If the room smells fusty, a bit doggy, of tobacco or even just a bit stale then open the windows, get some air flowing through and freshen the carpet using bicarb with cinnamon or lavender added (see pages 163–4).

Wipe down paintwork and light switches, removing any scuffs (see pages 187–9).

Vacuum floors and carpets, paying extra attention to corners and alongside skirting boards where the vacuum cleaner often cannot reach.

Mop hard floors and tiles. Again, pay extra attention to corners and alongside skirting boards where you may see spots of fly poop. You will know it when you see it – white windowsills and corners of hard floors will have tiny little black and brown spots the size of a pinhead. It can be stubborn to move, but a spray of all-purpose cleaner followed by a damp mop or cloth and it will lift off. I've read that it is speculated house flies defecate every time they land! Remember to keep food covered.

EVERY THREE TO SIX MONTHS

Clean the oven – once after Christmas and once in late summer (see pages 88–91).

Clean the hob and burners (see pages 92–4).

Clean the washing machine, though if you switch to a clean and green life, this will be a quick wipe and check over of the drum and detergent compartment. If you have moved house or a deeper clean is required, see pages 21–4. Try to get into the habit of leaving the washing machine door and detergent drawer slightly open when not in use. Air circulation will prevent any odours and build-up of mould.

Clean the dishwasher (see pages 82–4), checking and cleaning the filter, running a cleaning cycle. As with the washing machine, try to leave the door slightly ajar when not in use to prevent any odour building up, and if your dishwasher is used infrequently, run a rinse cycle every day or two.

Freshen the vacuum cleaner – checking and cleaning the filter as per manufacturer's instructions (see page 179).

Clean the fridge – check the drainage hole, check the seals for signs of mould and mildew (see pages 117–19).

Clean the microwave (see pages 95–6).

Deep clean of toilet to remove any limescale build-up (see pages 196–201).

Clean shower screen or curtain and check for mould or mildew (see pages 108–9, 202–4).

Check shower rose, sinks and bath and spot-treat limescale if necessary (see pages 205–6).

Check taps, fittings and bathroom furniture for limescale build-up and treat as necessary (see pages 207–9).

Clean and treat wooden kitchen utensils and chopping boards (see pages 97–9).

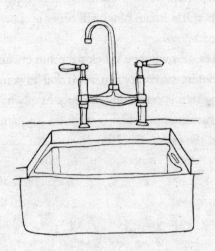

EVERY MONTH

Clean outside windows (see pages 134–6).

Check outside drains and clear of debris, especially in the autumn when leaves can block fall pipes and prevent effective drainage.

Check supplies of your own cleaning products and order up new supplies as necessary (so annoying if you go to start the cleaning to first have to make up a supply of all-purpose cleaner or furniture polish).

Descale the kettle (see pages 106–7).

EVERY WEEK OR TWO WEEKS

Clean each room by polishing surfaces and vacuuming and/or mopping floors.

Clean bathroom, toilets and shower (see pages 108–9, 196–201).

Wash cleaning cloths (see pages 55–7).

EVERY DAY

Clean the kitchen sink (see pages 111–12).
Clean the dishcloths (see pages 55–7).
Clean the toilets (see pages 197–8).

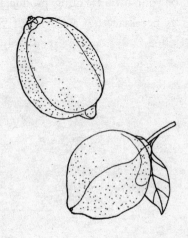

THANK YOU

Thank you for reading, and I hope feeling inspired to join me on my clean and green journey. These tips, recipes and methods have been proven to work for me. At the time of writing it has been nearly three years since I made the switch. Just small steps to begin with, but then as my followers became more engaged the cleaning challenges got bigger, which meant I had to get creative, experimenting and working tirelessly until I got to the point where the results were good enough. I wish I had a collection of video out-takes where my disasters were recorded. The time I sprayed every downstairs room in the house with my state-of-the-art room freshener which covered everything in white splashes, or my rufty-tufty floor cleaner that resulted in shoes and slippers sticking to the floor.

Those of you who have made changes will agree that the whole experience becomes addictive. Making one change feels good, and you will want to do more. I now realize that the old ways are not in fact inferior to chemical alternatives, and for so many cleaning jobs they are actually better.

Since going green I spend much less money on cleaning and household products. Trying to quantify that is difficult because I now shop differently. Instead of including on my weekly shopping list laundry detergents, fabric conditioner, bathroom cleaners, floor cleaners, kitchen cleaners, toilet cleaners, wood polish, silver and brass cleaners, air fresheners, laundry starch, teak oil, shoe polish, single-use wipes and bleach – the list goes on and on – I have instead a number of staple ingredients on my cleaning shelf that I buy in larger quantities.

For example, instead of 15g single-use sachets of bicarb I buy 5kg tubs and a 200ml bottle of white vinegar is now replaced by a 5-litre container. Surgical spirit, washing soda and citric acid now take pride of place on my cleaning shelf. My store cupboard cleaning staples then come together in a variety of simple recipes to do all of the cleaning jobs around my house. There is a list of ingredients and equipment at the beginning of the book. Once you have these, you are equipped to clean just about anything.

There are a growing number of eco-friendly cleaning products entering the market, but when writing this book I was mindful that in order to make the switch the cost has to be at least the same or (even better) less than even the basics in the supermarket. My recipes do that. How much you spend on cleaning products will be substantially reduced, the recipes and tips work and you will have fun.

Not only have I reduced the cost of my household cleaning considerably, but I have also cut my single-use packaging waste, single-use plastic consumption and fundamentally and most importantly, I am proud to no longer be adding to the amount of pollutants currently being absorbed by our planet.

Let us keep doing what we do. I have never enjoyed dancing my way through cleaning more than I do now!

Nancy

Acknowledgements

This book has been several years in the writing. What started off as a few scribbled notes in my page-a-day diary, to now a collection of 101 tips in a beautiful book seems unbelievable. I am super proud of this piece of work which has seen every emotion in me; frustration, fatigue, fun, fear and now friendship. I adore this book.

There are a number of people I would like to thank because without them this book could not have materialised.

My Publisher and friends at One Boat books – in particular Hockley. You've heard the saying 'both singing from the same hymn sheet'? – well this was certainly the case. From the outset, both publisher and author had a shared vision of the finished product and from the first exchange of manuscript I felt supported, empowered and yet ever so gently steered back on course when I tended to go off-piste!

My agents and friends at Yellow Poppy Media. They have supported, advised and sign-posted me for the past six years and continue to instil in me the fact that quality counts. This fantastic team have an amazing ability to know what is exactly right for me, they know my strengths (and many weaknesses) and are always there to help, facilitate and manage my work.

My followers – for whom without their continued support,

engagement and encouragement I doubt I would have had the energy to write a second book. Eco-friendly cleaning tips and recipes are really popular and I would like to thank those followers who have offered up and shared their own cleaning tips. There are those too that have revelled in and shared my green cleaning ways and those that have presented me with cleaning questions of their own. This 'problem solving' has been fantastic because in order to a present solution it involved me having to research, concoct and experiment until I could come up effective alternatives to the use of harmful chemicals. This has broadened my knowledge and enabled me to make the book as wide-ranging as it is.

A special mention to Emma Mitchell who, being a botanist, became quite involved in my work and the 'back to nature' type cleaning ways. We met through social media and face to face on screen. We get on so well and she then wrote an amazing foreword to this book – her writing is warm and easy to read – wish I could write just like Emma.

I am absolutely over the moon with the comments from early reviewers of this book. Can you believe this small person from the north of England has impacted on the cleaning routines of such famous names? I am speechless – which is a rare occurrence!

My family members and friends – they are always there for me though I know there have been times when they have thought I was going completely round the bend. When they visit and see lemon halves stuck on the end of taps or I'm dancing around the kitchen shaking rice in the bottom of stained vases like a pair of maracas, or I could have just returned home and be emptying my pockets of conkers which I tell them will be turned into liquid detergent. I know them all well enough to read their thoughts – simply from the raised eyebrows and heavy sighs!

Last and by no means least – him indoors! (Tim). My clean and green journey started off as a battle and it took some considerable time to persuade the person with whom I live to understand and accept that this is what we were going to do. This was the last straw! I recall a fairly heated discussion over chlorine bleach. I suggested he explain to the youngest grandchild that Grannie had made an alternative product which will clean the loo safely and effectively but that Grandpa chooses to use the one that will kill all the fishes. He was converted.

Tim is a huge support – quietly getting on in the background with all the paperwork, computer work and generally 'carrying the load'. I recall a moan when I mentioned having to carry my cleaning bottles around the house was a bind and secretly he made me the most adorable carrying case out of recycled wood and surplus chalk paint. I love it (and him)!

Author biography

Nancy Birtwhistle is a Hull-born baker who won the fifth series of *The Great British Bake Off* in 2014. Nancy worked as a GP practice manager in the NHS for thirty-six years until she retired in 2007. Motivated by protecting the planet for her ten grandchildren, Nancy decided to change how she used plastic, single-use products and chemicals in her home. Sharing her tips online, she amassed an engaged international following of devoted fans interested not only in her delicious recipes, but also her innovative ideas and time-saving swaps that rethink everyday household chores to make as little an impact on the environment as possible.

Connect with Nancy on Instagram: @nancy.birtwhistle, on Twitter: @nancybbakes or through her website: nancybirtwhistle.co.uk

Index

TEN MORE TIPS!

For this paperback edition of *Clean & Green* I just couldn't help but add in the extra tips I've developed since the hardback book published back in 2021. I hope you find them as useful as I do!

1. SPRUCE UP YOUR VINEGAR

White vinegar is used widely throughout this book and whether cleaning the washing machine, making up a bottle of fabric softener, all-purpose cleaner, floor cleaner, pet deterrent spray or to use simply as a solution to remove tea and coffee spills (and just about any other stain) from carpets – that pungent vinegar smell needn't put you off.

Vinegar is now being sold as a natural cleaning product in its own right, though manufacturers are often infusing it often with citrus to make the smell more pleasing (and then increasing the price for the sweet-smelling privilege).

However, you can easily make your own. Cleaning vinegar can be 'spruced' up in just a couple of days, costs next to nothing and can then go on to replace essential oil if required.

You will need

2–3 sprigs cut from a spruce (Christmas) tree
1 litre jar with lid
Discarded orange peels, enough to fill the jar
700ml white vinegar (or sufficient to fill the jar)
Measuring jug

Pop the spruce sprigs into the jar then pack it tightly with discarded orange peels. Fill the jar with vinegar, screw the top on and leave to infuse for a minimum of 3 days. Pour off the bright orange, sweet-pine-perfumed vinegar into a measuring jug and use in your favourite cleaning recipes. I have used the peels several times before discarding, but if the spruce has discoloured I remove it.

2. POLISH OFF THE PRICE TAGS

The sticky label remover on page 104 is great for used jars that are to be recycled for jams, chutneys and the like – but is too oily for removing labels on certain items (for example, those to be given as gifts).

Many labels will lift, peel and can be removed easily, but then there are the others that seem as though they are doing just fine, yet you can be left with a thin film of sticky paper or glue.

The good news is that the remnants of such a label can be removed quickly and easily without the need for harmful solvents.

You will need

Soft cotton pad (I use a reusable makeup pad)
Surgical spirit (rubbing alcohol)

Simply dampen the pad with the spirit then apply to the sticky area and the adhesive paper or residual adhesive will just easily wipe away. The surgical spirit evaporates almost immediately taking away any sign of the price tag!

Brilliant to use on glass, pottery and stiff cardboard.

3. CLEANING OUT CANDLE HOLDERS

Many people exchange candles as gifts at holidays and birthdays. I adore them – coloured, scented and many in the most beautiful jars and containers.

Once they have burned down and are well past their former glory – what to do with them and how to remove the candle residue? And can the wax be reused?

I have cleaned up many glass jars to then reuse as vases, trinket holders and a particularly gorgeous one that matches the colour of my bathroom is used to store soap slivers for making the best laundry detergent (see page 000).

Spent candle holders can be placed into the freezer. The wax then hardens and can be broken with the round blade of a knife and lifted out of the jar or glass in hard pieces. I found that any fine film continued to adhere to the side of the glass – my favourite way is to melt the wax.

You will need

Saucepan large enough to hold the candle holders
Cloth to stand in the bottom of the pan
Used candle holders containing wax remnants
Water
Kitchen paper or newspaper
Empty tin can or silicone mould
Oven glove

Take the saucepan and lay the cloth at the bottom – this will prevent the candle holders from cracking or banging together. Pour water into the pan, around the outside of the candle holders, to reach about 2.5cm (1 inch) up the side of them.

Heat gently over a low flame until you see the wax melt and turn clear – the water doesn't need to boil.

Use a gloved hand to remove each candle holder from the water and pour the liquid wax (and the remains of the candle wick) into a clean, empty tin can or silicone mould. Remove the wick and discard. Use kitchen paper or scrunched newspaper to wipe around the inside of the holder to ensure all wax residue is removed.

Wash in hot soapy water and repeat the process for the remaining candle holders.

4. BOOT AND SHOE WEATHER-PROOFER WAX

Treat those much-loved hard-working boots or shoes to a fresh weather-proofing wax layer.

You can use the wax collected from spent candle holders (see page 294) as a free treatment for shoes and boots.

Winter weather will take its toll on our outdoor footwear. My favourite black working boots which are so comfy but had started to let water in across a crease in the top were soon sorted using this method. The treatment not only made them weatherproof – raindrops just ran off – but also made them look ten years younger!

You will need

Leather boots or shoes
2–3 tbsp white vinegar
2–3 drops eco-friendly washing up liquid/dish soap
Small bowl of warm water
Cloth for washing
Cloth for drying
A spent candle or piece of recycled wax (see page 294)
Hairdryer
Old towel and soft cloth

Start by removing any laces from the shoes or boots. Add the vinegar and eco-friendly washing up liquid to a bowl of warm water, and use the cloth dipped in this cleaning solution to wash the shoes or boots. Clean them up completely, removing any dried-on mud, stains or dirt.

Use a dry cloth to mop up excess moisture then leave the footwear to dry naturally and completely.

When ready to treat I lay out an old towel on a work surface, place my clean, dry footwear on the towel then take the wax piece and rub all over the boots or shoes into every nook and cranny. The finished footwear needs to look speckled all over in wax. Mine looked as though they were covered in frost!

Take then the hairdryer and blow the hot air onto the boots. The wax will immediately melt and soak into the leather. I use the soft cloth to then evenly distribute it and massage in.

Thread through the laces (don't forget to clean them as well!) and your boots or shoes are rejuvenated.

5. LIQUID LAUNDRY DETERGENT

I find a liquid laundry soap is more effective than powder or flakes, especially when washing at low temperatures. Soap powder or flakes may leave a residue on dark fabrics whereas a liquid readily dissolves. I now wash laundry on a long two-hour eco cycle at just 20 degrees. I absolutely recommend you give it a try – it has been a life changer for me.

There are natural detergents, but Conker detergent on page 33 and Ivy detergent on page 31 may not be accessible to everyone: maybe there isn't the time to be foraging around before doing the laundry. With the reliance and inevitability of yet another plastic bottle when buying even an eco-friendly plant-based detergent, I had to come up with an effective, affordable option and here it is.

Save your soap slivers, use a vegan bar, single use hotel soaps or any plant based soap and we can make our own eco-friendly laundry detergent. Avoid lemon scented soaps because they can cause splitting because the acid reacts with the washing soda.

You will need

Hand blender with attachment, fine grater or sharp knife
Kettle of boiling water
Cold water
Large bowl or jug
Wooden spoon or spatula
2 x 1 litre plastic bottles with lids
75g solid vegan soap (or use slivers or single use hotel soaps),
   not lemon scented
75g Washing soda crystals (sodium carbonate)
10ml eco-friendly washing up liquid/dish soap
10 drops organic essential oil for perfume (optional) – try lavender
500ml boiling water
1300ml cold water

The soap needs to be either grated or blitzed to a powder using a hand blender. If using slivers I find it easier to blitz, but a bar of soap is easier if you simply cut off small shards.

Transfer the measured soap powder into a large bowl or jug then stir in 500ml boiling water and stir until the soap dissolves. Add the washing soda and essential oil if using.

The washing soda can seem to go lumpy in the hot water to begin with but keep stirring until it dissolves. I used a hand blender to ensure the mixture was smooth.

Add the 1300ml cold water, stir then set aside. The liquid is very thin at this stage.

As the soap cools it will thicken, but if it becomes too thick to pour (some soaps thicken more than others) then add more cold water to achieve a thick pouring consistency.

Pour into the 1 litre bottles, label and use about 100ml per wash cycle. I have a plastic measuring cup that holds the exact amount that I can then pop directly into the drum. Add 2–3 tbsp washing soda into the detergent drawer and fabric softener as described on page 35.

6. CONCENTRATED HAND-WASH DETERGENT

Small single-use, costly plastic bottles of holiday 'travel wash' detergent can be a thing of the past as we can mix our own concentrated blend to activate by adding warm water once on holiday. This simple, inexpensive detergent is easy to make and is very effective for dissolving any stains from sun oils and creams, fake tan or makeup.

You will need

Processor or coffee grinder
Digital scales
Funnel
500ml recycled plastic bottle with screw top
15g Soap slivers
20g Washing Soda
4 drops eco friendly washing up liquid/dish soap
450ml warm water

Weigh the soap slivers and break into the bowl of a small processor or coffee grinder. Add the measured amount of washing soda then blitz to a fine powder. Use the funnel to decant into the bottle then add the washing up liquid. Replace the cap then pack along with holiday clothes. No fear of leaks or spills.

Once on holiday fill the bottle with hand-hot water, replace the cap and shake to mix. Use 2–3 tbsp to a bowl to hand-wash swimwear or undies while on holiday. Leaving soiled items soaking overnight in a measure of soap and tepid water will dissolve sun creams and oils.

7. HEAT RING ELIMINATOR

I love the festive season. The house can be filled with people young and old, out comes the best china, cutlery and glassware. Cooking, baking and food galore – the squeals from young children getting over-excited and hot as they run around having fun.

It is impossible to keep a watchful eye on everything and when, after the crowds have gone and all is cleared away, I spot a collection of white heat rings on my wooden table from hot mugs of tea or coffee . . . I know all is not lost.

You will need

Warm damp cloth
Bicarbonate of soda
Clean old thick towel
Iron (with steam setting)

If the heat ring is not too pronounced it may be possible to make it disappear using a warm damp cloth. A cloth rinsed in hot water then wrung out well so it is just damp, then dipped into dry bicarbonate of soda can clear the stain. Rub in the direction of the grain.

If this doesn't hit the spot then take an old thick towel and lay it over the white ring. With the iron on and set to the steam setting, carefully position the iron over the towel above the ring. Start slowly and hover the iron over for only a second, remove the towel and examine – repeating as necessary until the heat ring has disappeared. If the heat ring fails to disappear then lightly place the iron actually onto the towel, a few seconds at a time.

It feels a bit scary to do, and slowly does it – but it works!

8. ALL-PURPOSE CLEANER FOR THOSE HARD-TO-REACH PLACES

This simple spray (see page 108) cuts through grease and grime, shines without streaking, dries quickly and is therefore perfect for mirrors, stainless steel, tiles and glass. However, attempting to clean glass light fittings or glass droplets and beads suspended from a light fitting with a spray is going to result in drips of cleaning liquid dripping everywhere, spraying where you don't want it and generally using much more cleaning product than is needed.

Add a pair of white cotton gloves to your cleaning materials and you can clean even the most intricate object in minutes.

Wearing a pair of white cotton gloves, spray the palm and fingers of each hand with the all-purpose cleaner. With the dampened gloves on, work your hands around the moving parts of the light fitting or chandelier, using the dampened fingers to get into every nook and cranny. You will be surprised by the amount of dust and dirt that immediately lifts off leaving clean sparkly glass, chains and any hanging elements. Once the palm side of the gloves is grubby – simply swap gloves – moving the left glove to the right hand and vice versa. The dirty side then transfers to the back of the hands, providing two clean palm and finger sides.

9. EVERLASTING CANDLES

Large church candles are beautiful but expensive, adding a soft cosy glow to any room. I love them.

This little tip I picked up from a gorgeous hotel in Italy. The guest lounge was so pretty with candles everywhere, a log fire, rugs, cosy sofas and cushions. Wherever I sat I would see candlelight reflected in mirrors, wine glasses, polished wood and windows.

I remember thinking 'these candles must cost a fortune,' when I saw that each night the candles were new, tall and fresh. Not a burned-down candle in sight.

Then I noted the secret. A new light was indeed lit every night but on close inspection I realised this was in fact a small tea light counter-sunk into the main tall candle. 'Genius!' I thought, making a mental note to try it myself.

You will need

Tweezers

Round metal biscuit or pastry cutter of the same diameter as the tea lights

Heat source

Oven glove

Large master candles

Round-ended knife

Metal teaspoon

Small scissors

Good-quality tea lights with several hours burning time

Use the tweezers to hold the metal cutter and heat over a flame. I use a gas flame then when you think the cutter is hot centre it over the wick of the main candle. You will know whether the cutter is hot enough because it will immediately sink into the wax. If not heat a minute longer.

Press down on the hot cutter using an oven glove or similar until it is bedded down into the wax to a depth the same as the tea light to be used.

Use the round-ended knife and / or teaspoon to scrape out the wax from the centre of the cutter. The wax will have softened from the heat from the cutter and can be spooned out leaving the exposed wick which can be trimmed using the scissors.

Once the wax has been removed, lift out the cutter then drop a tea light into the hole.

Make sure the tea light sits just below the surface of the hole and if not remove a little more wax.

Your large church candles can be replenished each night with a small tea light – never to burn down – to last evermore.

10. THE BEST BATH BOMBS

Always to be counted on as a reliable gift or stocking filler – the bath bombs! Shop-bought versions can work out expensive and there is always the inevitable single-use plastic packaging. Children love them, as do adults and they are very easy to make at home.

There are many recipes available but when I examined then went on to try and test some of them, I felt they lacked a professional look, being a bit crumbly, rough in texture with an uneven mottled colour.

My recipe overcomes all of the above and the finished article is smooth, even-coloured and firm – and they work. Pop one into the bath, see it fizz and bubble then enjoy the water which is soft and soothing: the oil softens the skin and your favourite perfume permeates the room.

These bombs make the perfect gift and need only to be wrapped in tissue paper, secured with a pretty sticker then enclosed in a home-made paper gift box.

You will need

Small non-metallic container for coconut oil
Microwave
Silicone moulds – I use teacake moulds and this recipe makes 8
Food processor with blade attachment
Spatula
Teaspoon
Digital weighing scales
100g Coconut oil

200g Bicarbonate of soda

100g Citric Acid

100g Epsom Salt

100g Cornflour

10–15 drops organic essential oil or food flavour extract for scent

15–20 drops food or soap colour

Begin by melting the coconut oil. I use the microwave and 30 second blasts until the oil is melted but not too hot. Set aside.

Place the bowl of the food processor onto the scales and weigh directly into the bowl the bicarbonate of soda (water softener), citric acid (fizzer), Epsom salt (softens rough, dry skin), the cornflour (binding agent), essential oil (scent) and your chosen food or soap colour.

Blitz until the mixture develops a fine powder and is pale in colour. (The colour will darken in the next step when you add the oil.)

With the machine running, pour in the melted coconut oil (to bind the mix and soften the skin) in a thin, steady stream and the mix will begin to clump slightly and darken in colour.

Spoon the mix into the silicone moulds and press down firmly with the back of the teaspoon. The finish needs to look smooth and flawless.

Leave to set in a cool place or the fridge for at least an hour or until the bombs feel very firm. Turn out of the silicone moulds.

To present them as boxed gifts simply wrap neatly in tissue paper, secure with a sticker and pop into a presentation box.

Activate in hot water at bath time!

Notes